TO BID OR
NOT TO BID

LARRY COHEN

MASTER POINT PRESS

In memory of Nathan Cohen

Thanks to
Randy Baron, Marty Bergen, David Berkowitz, Kitty Bethe, Herb Cohen, Jon Cohen, Neil Cohen, Paul Cohen, Susie Cohen, Allan Falk, Harold Feldheim, Thomas Goodwin, Matthew Granovetter, Mike Lawrence, Eric Leong, Pat Lilly, Edwin Kantar, Robin Kay, Alex McCallum, Eric Rodwell, Om Sundar Sayenju, Paul Shapiro, Stan Sterenberg, Frank Stewart, Alan Truscott, and Steve Weinstein

Master Point Press
331 Douglas Ave.
Toronto, Ontario Canada
M5M 1H2   (416) 781-0351
Email   info@masterpointpress.com
Websites   www.masterpointpress.com
               www.masteringbridge.com
               www.bridgeblogging.com
               www.ebooksbridge.com

Canadian Cataloguing in Publication Data
Cohen, Larry, 1959-
To bid or not to bid: the LAW of total tricks

ISBN 978-1-894154-48-2

1. Contract bridge — Bidding I. Title
GV1282.4.C64 2002   795.41'52 C2002-901833-1

Editor   Karen MacCullum
Cover and Interior design   Olena S. Sullivan
Interior format and copyediting Deanna Bourassa

Printed and bound in Canada by Webcom

3 4 5 6 7 8   13 12 11 10 09

Contents

FOREWORD

June, 1969, was an important month in my life. I got married, moved into a new apartment, graduated college and read a bridge article.

What's the big deal about the bridge article? If anyone had told me that there was something in my mailbox which would have a dramatic effect on my life, I'd have called the bomb squad! But, there was no one to warn me, so all I knew was that my monthly Bridge World had arrived. My bridge life would never be the same...

The article, entitled *The Law of Total Tricks* by Jean René Vernes, suggested a revolutionary idea. According to Verne, in the area of competitive bidding, trumps are everything! I was fascinated by the idea. I read and reread the article countless times. It was a revelation. I couldn't wait to test it out at the table. And I loved to pore through hand records after the session to observe the Law of Total Tricks in action. Although it didn't take long for me to become a believer, I've never ceased to be impressed by its accuracy.

It annoyed me in those days to be repeatedly confronted with the puzzling behavior of other expert players. They reacted quite differently to what, by then, had become simply the 'LAW' to my now obedient bridge brain. For the most part, they were unwilling to go along with the idea. Instead, they stubbornly preferred to back their judgment. Fortunately, for me, more of them were opponents than partners.

In 1979, another important milestone... I met Larry Cohen, who was to become one of my best friends and most successful bridge partners. Larry was captivated by the Law of Total Tricks, just as I had been ten years before. Our partnership methods were designed specifically to utilize the principles dictated by the LAW. He became an eager disciple, and a skilled practitioner.

Larry and I both have preached the LAW ever since, whenever a chance happens to present itself — writing, lecturing and teaching the concepts to anyone who will listen. We've been nothing less than delighted to have discovered a simple and effective tool which serves to make certain bridge decisions trivial. The time to share the secrets with bridge players everywhere is long overdue.

Larry has set down the principles in a clear, orderly and concise manner, with realistic suggestions on how to incorporate LAW ideas into your own bidding methods. A serious reader will derive a great deal of usable knowledge if he takes it to heart.

Larry's book won't do anything to help your card play - there's not a backwash squeeze to be found. But then, you're not likely to encounter one of those at the table anytime soon. What you will see, every time you play, are innumerable competitive bidding decisions. The practical advice contained in these pages will help you get those right — time after time. Obey the LAW and make winning decisions — that's what To Bid or Not to Bid is all about.

Marty Bergen
May, 1992

INTRODUCTION

To bid or not to bid. That is the question faced in every competitive auction. Should I sell out to the opponents, or bid one more? Should I defend, or try to win the contract for our side? I first became aware of the concepts discussed in this book back in 1979, when I met the prolific Marty Bergen at the Cincinnati Fall Nationals. Always eager to share his original ideas, Marty monopolized the dinner conversation for several hours, expounding upon his personal favorite — the Law of Total Tricks. I was hooked.

Several years later, Marty and I started our partnership and based our entire system upon the Law of Total Tricks. More than anything else, I attribute our successes of the 1980's to the LAW. Sure, we're both good card players and good constructive bidders, but so are thousands of other experts. What most helped us win seven National Championships as partners was our competitive decisions.

In this modern era of bridge, opponents very rarely give your side a free run in the bidding. Most decisions have to be made in competition — often after preempts. To rely solely on judgment is unpleasant at best. The world's best frequently go wrong when faced with competitive bidding decisions. Because the opponents have taken away the bidding room, it often boils down to nothing more than guesswork.

Fortunately, for Marty and me, we didn't have to rely on judgment or guesswork. We let the Law of Total Tricks make our competitive decisions, and found it to be far superior to any bridge player's judgment.

Experts are renowned for their big egos. They believe that no law can substitute for experience and a keen sense of evaluation and deduction. What they don't realize is that the Law of Total Tricks is at the foundation of every bridge deal, and is far more accurate than their judgement.

I want to share the LAW with not only the disdaining experts, but with bridge players at every-level, including beginners. If I were to teach bridge to a novice, I would consider the Law of Total Tricks to be a fundamental concept — imperative learning material.

The definition of the LAW, and how it works, is the subject of the first chapter. In Chapter Two, you will begin to see why the LAW is of utmost importance in a competitive auction.

If any player were to read only those two chapters, I can promise that his or her bridge game would improve dramatically. However, there are many fine points as well as corollaries to the LAW. The rest of the book is devoted to fine-tuning. At the end, I've included a chapter on World Championship decisions where the Law of Total Tricks came into play (or should have).

I believe that the Law of Total Tricks will revolutionize the way bridge players bid in competition. Such is my belief that I fear that too many people will read this book, and make the right decision the next time they sit down to play at my table.

Larry Cohen

WHAT IS THE LAW?

CHAPTER 1

1978...NEW ORLEANS – WORLD PAIR OLYMPIAD

Brazilian star, Marcello Branco, was well on his way to winning the World Pairs Championship when he picked up:

♠ A K Q 8 6   ♡ 10 7 6 3   ◇ J 8   ♣ A 10

With nobody vulnerable he dealt and opened the bidding with one spade. After a two heart overcall, he was raised to two spades. His right hand opponent jumped to four hearts and it was up to him:

Branco	Oppt.	Cintra	Oppt.
1♠	2♡	2♠	4♡
??			

Can you make a better decision than Branco made? By the time you reach the end of Chapter Two you'll know what to do.*

The Law of Total Tricks can best be understood by first looking at a very ordinary bridge deal:

```
                    ♠ K Q J 2
                    ♡ K Q 3
                    ◇ 8 5 4
                    ♣ 8 6 2
    ♠ 8 5                           ♠ 6 4 3
    ♡ 8 6 5          N              ♡ 9 7 4 2
    ◇ K Q 2      W       E          ◇ J 10 6
    ♣ A J 10 4 3      S             ♣ K Q 7
                    ♠ A 10 9 7
                    ♡ A J 10
                    ◇ A 9 7 3
                    ♣ 9 5
```

On this deal, North-South will probably play in spades, and take nine tricks (losing two tricks in each minor suit). If East-West were to play the hand in clubs, they would take seven tricks (losing two spades, three hearts, and the ace of diamonds).

---

* It's too early to explain how the LAW would guide you to the winning decision. If you simply must know the answer now, see page 33.

Even though both sides can't play the hand at the same time, we will, for argument's sake, say that on this deal there are **16 total tricks** — North-South have nine tricks in spades, and East-West have seven tricks in clubs.

Now, let's look at how many trumps there are in this deal. North-South, if they play in spades, have eight trumps. East-West, if they play in clubs, also have eight trumps. Even though both suits can't be trump at the same time, we will again, for argument's sake, say that on this deal there are **16 total trumps** — eight for North-South in spades, and eight for East-West in clubs.

Is it a coincidence that there are 16 *total tricks* and 16 *total trumps*? Not at all. In fact, this phenomenon is the basis for the Law of Total Tricks, and the entire contents of this book.

> The Total Number of Tricks available on any deal
>
> is approximately equal to the
>
> Total Number of Trumps.

Using its simplest definition, The Law of Total Tricks states: **Total Number of Tricks** means the combined Total Tricks available to both sides (assuming best play and defense) if they play in their best (longest) fit. For example, if North-South can take ten tricks in their 5-4 (longest) spade fit, and East-West can take seven tricks in their 4-4 (longest) diamond fit, then the Total Number of Tricks would be 10+7, or 17.

Total Number of Trumps means the combined total of cards in both sides' best trump fit. For example, if North-South's best (longest) fit is a 5-4 spade fit, and East-West's best (longest) fit is a 4-4 diamond fit, then the Total Number of Trumps would be 9+8, or 17.

If North-South's longest fit is ten cards, and East-West's longest fit is nine cards, then the LAW says that there are 19 Total Tricks available. Those 19 tricks can be divided in many different ways — maybe North-South can take 11, and East-West can take eight — or vice versa — but the *Total Number of Tricks* is fixed at 19.

1980...VALKENBURG – WORLD TEAM OLYMPIAD

You're representing Brazil, and vulnerable against not you're holding

♠ A Q 7 6 2   ♡ A   ◇ A 7 6 3   ♣ 10 9 6

In second seat you open with one spade, and hear the following auction:

Rodrigue	Branco	Priday	You
		pass	1♠
2♣	2♡	3♣	3◇
4♣	4♠	5♣	??

This was the difficult decision faced by the Brazilian player, Gabino Cintra. What do your instincts tell you to do? Midway through Chapter Two you'll *know* what to do.*

Let's study a few deals and see the LAW at work:

```
                    ♠ K J 5
                    ♡ A Q 10 8
                    ◇ Q J 10
                    ♣ K 4 2
    ♠ 8 7 6          ┌─────────┐        ♠ A Q 3 2
    ♡ 5 4 3          │    N    │        ♡ K 6
    ◇ 9 8 3          │ W     E │        ◇ K 4 2
    ♣ A Q 10 6       │    S    │        ♣ J 9 8 7
                    └─────────┘
                    ♠ 10 9 4
                    ♡ J 9 7 2
                    ◇ A 7 6 5
                    ♣ 5 3
```

In this example, North-South's longest fit is eight hearts, and East-West's longest fit is eight clubs, for a total of 16 trumps. The LAW says that there should be 16 tricks.

---

*If you can't wait, see page 37.

Are there? In hearts, North-South lose two spades, one heart, and one club — so they can take nine tricks. East-West have three diamond losers and one loser in every other suit, so they can take seven tricks with clubs trump. North-South can take nine tricks, East-West can take seven, for a total of 16 tricks — equal to the 16 trumps.

Does it seem like all of those winning and losing finesses were set up just right to make the example work? Let's see what happens if we change things around by moving some of the important cards.

Let's start by completely interchanging the East and West hands to make the layout:

```
                    ♠ K J 5
                    ♡ A Q 10 8
                    ◇ Q J 10
                    ♣ K 4 2
      ♠ A Q 3 2      ┌───────────┐      ♠ 8 7 6
      ♡ K 6          │     N     │      ♡ 5 4 3
      ◇ K 4 2        │ W       E │      ◇ 9 8 3
      ♣ J 9 8 7      │     S     │      ♣ A Q 10 6
                     └───────────┘
                    ♠ 10 9 4
                    ♡ J 9 7 2
                    ◇ A 7 6 5
                    ♣ 5 3
```

North-South still can take nine tricks in hearts (this time losing one spade, one diamond, and two clubs), and East-West will take seven tricks in clubs (losing two spades, two hearts, and two diamonds). There are still 16 Total Tricks.

Working with this 'interchanged' diagram, let's trade West's king of hearts for East's three, so that the heart finesse becomes favorable for East-West:

```
              ♠ K J 5
              ♡ A Q 10 8
              ◇ Q J 10
              ♣ K 4 2
♠ A Q 3 2        ┌─────────┐        ♠ 8 7 6
♡ 6 3            │    N    │        ♡ K 5 4
◇ K 4 2          │ W     E │        ◇ 9 8 3
♣ J 9 8 7        │    S    │        ♣ A Q 10 6
                 └─────────┘
              ♠ 10 9 4
              ♡ J 9 7 2
              ◇ A 7 6 5
              ♣ 5 3
```

Now North-South can take only eight tricks in hearts — but the Total Trick count is still 16 because East-West can take eight tricks in clubs.

Try switching some other key cards and you'll see that the total tricks will remain at 16. By interchanging cards, all you're really doing is making a finesse lose for one side, but making it win for the other — i.e. one side has one more trick, one side has one less trick, but the total number of tricks never changes.

1979...RIO DE JANIERO – BERMUDA BOWL

You're holding

♠ J 9 3   ♡ Q 8 6   ◇ A 7 4 3   ♣ A 5 3

at favorable vulnerability. The colossal champion of the illustrious Blue Team, Giorgio Belladonna, on your left, opens one diamond. Your partner overcalls one heart, and your right hand opponent bids one spade. You raise only to two hearts, and are soon faced with:

Passell	Belladonna	Brachman	Pittala
	1◇	1♡	1♠
2♡	3♣	pass	pass
??			

Can you avoid the error made by the consummate professional, American expert Mike Passell? This kind of decision will no longer be a problem for you when you get through Chapter Two.*

Let's now look at another deal:

```
                    ♠ 5 4 3
                    ♡ 8 7 2
                    ◇ A Q 7
                    ♣ K 10 9 7
  ♠ Q 10 9 2      ┌─────────┐      ♠ A K J
  ♡ A Q J 10 6    │    N    │      ♡ K 9 5 3
  ◇ 5 4           │ W     E │      ◇ 10 8 6 3
  ♣ 6 5           │    S    │      ♣ 3 2
                  └─────────┘
                    ♠ 8 7 6
                    ♡ 4
                    ◇ K J 9 2
                    ♣ A Q J 8 4
```

Here, North-South have nine trumps (clubs) and East-West have nine (hearts) for a total of 18 trumps. North-South can take nine tricks in clubs (losing three spades and one heart), while East-West have nine tricks in hearts (losing two in each minor) for a total of 18 tricks.

If you were to interchange West's ace of hearts with South's singleton four, it wouldn't affect the Total Trick count:

```
                    ♠ 5 4 3
                    ♡ 8 7 2
                    ◇ A Q 7
                    ♣ K 10 9 7
  ♠ Q 10 9 2      ┌─────────┐      ♠ A K J
  ♡ Q J 10 6 4    │    N    │      ♡ K 9 5 3
  ◇ 5 4           │ W     E │      ◇ 10 8 6 3
  ♣ 6 5           │    S    │      ♣ 3 2
                  └─────────┘
                    ♠ 8 7 6
                    ♡ A
                    ◇ K J 9 2
                    ♣ A Q J 8 4
```

---

*Full deal can be found on pages 40-42.

North-South would have ten tricks (still losing three spades, but no hearts). However, East-West now have only eight (losing the same four tricks as before and the ace of hearts). The addition becomes 10+8 instead of 9+9, but the total is still the same 18.

The total number of tricks isn't determined by the location of the high-cards, but simply by the total number of trumps. In the next chapter, we will start to see why we should care about this phenomenon. For now, we must simply understand what the LAW is and how it works. We'll look at why in the later chapters.

Following is a deal that illustrates, in a slightly different way, how the LAW works. We've seen that if a card is 'onside' for North-South, then it's 'offside' for East-West; therefore, the total number of tricks doesn't change. The same phenomenon occurs when looking at how the key suits are distributed:

```
                    ♠ J 10 8 2
                    ♡ J 10 7 4
                    ◇ 5 4
                    ♣ A K 5
  ♠ 7 5 3           ┌──────────┐      ♠ A 4
  ♡ 8 3             │    N     │      ♡ A 9 6 2
  ◇ K Q J 10 3 2    │ W     E  │      ◇ A 8 7
  ♣ 9 4             │    S     │      ♣ J 8 7 3
                    └──────────┘
                    ♠ K Q 9 6
                    ♡ K Q 5
                    ◇ 9 6
                    ♣ Q 10 6 2
```

Here, North-South have eight spades, and East-West have nine diamonds for 17 Total Trumps. Let's see if there are the expected 17 Total Tricks.

In diamonds, East-West must lose two tricks in clubs, along with one trick in each major. They can make nine tricks. In spades, North-South lose the two major suit aces, and two diamond tricks. Because of the 4-2 heart break, the defense can lead (or shift to) hearts, and obtain a ruff. This holds North-South to eight tricks. Eight for North-South, and nine for East-West make the expected total of 17 tricks.

Notice that the 4-2 heart break was needed to 'make the LAW work.' Or was it? As before, let's make a slight adjustment and see what happens to the LAW.

Previously, we switched the key high-cards and noted that the Total Trick count wasn't affected. In this case, we'll change the distribution of the heart suit and see what happens:

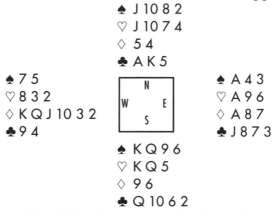

```
                    ♠ J 10 8 2
                    ♡ J 10 7 4
                    ♦ 5 4
                    ♣ A K 5
 ♠ 7 5                              ♠ A 4 3
 ♡ 8 3 2           N                ♡ A 9 6
 ♦ K Q J 10 3 2   W   E             ♦ A 8 7
 ♣ 9 4                S             ♣ J 8 7 3
                    ♠ K Q 9 6
                    ♡ K Q 5
                    ♦ 9 6
                    ♣ Q 10 6 2
```

Now the East-West hearts are divided 3-3, instead of 4-2, East-West can no longer obtain a heart ruff on defense. Consequently, North-South can now take nine tricks in spades, where before they could only take eight.

However, look what's happened to East-West's prospects in diamonds. They now have two heart losers, where they only had one before. They still lose a spade and two clubs, along with *two* hearts, and can now make only eight tricks.

The even heart split results in an additional trick for North-South, but one less trick for East-West. The Total Trick count is still 17 — this time it's nine for North-South and eight for East-West.

We have now seen illustrations of two factors which will not change the Total Trick count:

1) Location of high cards. Finesses that are onside for one pair will be offside for the other. **The Total Trick count is constant**.

2) Distribution of the suits. Bad breaks for one side translate into good breaks for the other. **The Total Trick count is constant**.

1979...RIO DE JANIERO – BERMUDA BOWL

You're representing Italy, sitting opposite Giorgio Belladonna. Vulnerable against not, you hold the following cards:

♠ K 9 7 3 2   ♡ 9 4   ◇ A Q 10   ♣ J 8 2 .

After two passes, the poker-faced American, Bobby Goldman, starts with one club on your left. Belladonna overcalls with one diamond, and Paul Soloway, the man with the most masterpoints, jumps preemptively to two hearts. You try two spades, and Goldman raises to three hearts which is passed around to you:

Goldman	Belladonna	Soloway	You
		pass	pass
1♣	1◇	2♡	2♠
3♡	pass	pass	??

Can you avoid the error made by Italian star, Vito Pittala? Yes, the solution is in Chapter Two.*

Now we'll look at one last deal which ties together all of the factors which define the Law of Total Tricks:

```
                    ♠ 7 6 4 2
                    ♡ A 9
                    ◇ 8 2
                    ♣ 10 9 5 3 2
    ♠ 9 3                              ♠ K Q J 10 8
    ♡ Q 5 4          N                ♡ J 6
    ◇ J 10 9 6 5   W   E              ◇ K 7 3
    ♣ K J 4          S                ♣ Q 7 6
                    ♠ A 5
                    ♡ K 10 8 7 3 2
                    ◇ A Q 4
                    ♣ A 8
```

---

* For the full deal see pages 44-45.

North-South can take ten tricks in hearts since they have no diamond losers (via a finesse and a third-round ruff), and only one loser in each other suit.

How many tricks can East-West take in diamonds? Only six against best defense. The defenders can take one spade trick, two heart tricks, two diamond tricks, one club trick and a club ruff, for seven tricks on defense.

North-South have ten tricks; East-West have six, for a total of 16 tricks equal to the 16 trumps.

It might seem that this deal is 'rigged' so that North-South can take all those tricks on defense, in order to make the LAW work out. Not true! The working diamond finesse, along with the distribution that allows North-South to take ten tricks in hearts, are the same features that allow them to take so many tricks on defense.

Again, the Total Trick Count is not based on where the key cards are located, nor on how the key suits split, but solely on the Total Number of Trumps.

In all of the examples so far, the LAW has been exactly right (Total Trumps = Total Tricks). In real life, this isn't always so. However, if the LAW isn't exactly right, it is normally off by only one — it is rare to find a deal where the LAW is off by two or more tricks. In Chapters Three and Nine there will be a discussion of when and why the LAW will be off, and how to allow for it during the bidding. For now, the key is to understand the basic workings of the LAW, and how to use this knowledge in the bidding — which is the subject matter of the next chapter.

Before reading ahead, you may wish to pick up any bridge magazine or book and look at deals from the point of view of the Law of Total Tricks. Alternatively, you may want to deal out a deck of cards and see how many trumps and tricks there are on each deal.

You'll find that some deals are too difficult to analyze, either because the 'best' line of play and defense is too hard to determine, or because it's just too complicated to figure out how many tricks each side should take. So, just skip over those hands for now and look at the simpler deals. Don't get discouraged if you find that the LAW is off on some deals. There is one major adjustment factor (along with many minor ones) which will be explained in Chapter Nine. We have only covered the basic definition so far, and using just that basic definition you can't realistically expect to find Total Trumps equal to Total Tricks on every deal.

Think of it this way — when you first learned to play, you were taught how to count your high-card points. You were told that 13 is an opening bid, etc. Later on, they told you how to 'adjust' for distribution, by adding points for short suits and/or long suits. So far, you've been told only how to count high-card points — we'll fine-tune the LAW later on.

CHAPTER REVIEW

- The Law of Total Tricks states that the Total Number of Tricks available on any deal is equal approximately to the Total Number of Trumps.

- To determine the Total Number of Trumps, count the cards in each side's longest trump fit.

- To obtain the Total Number of Tricks, see how many tricks each side can take, with best play and defense.

- The location of the high-cards and distribution of the suits will not affect the total number of tricks. Switching cards around tends to add a trick to one side's total, but to subtract a trick from the other side's, thereby keeping the total number of tricks unchanged.

- Look at deals in magazines, books, newspapers and analyze them from a LAW point of view. Some deals will be too hard to analyze, and on some deals the LAW will not work exactly.

- Be patient — later on in the book the fine-tuning of the LAW will be explained. For now, just get familiar with the basic definition of the LAW.

- The next chapter will begin to illustrate the practical value of the Law of Total Tricks.

1) The following diagrams intentionally show only distribution. It doesn't matter what the actual cards are in each suit — determine how many Total Tricks there will be on each layout:

a)

```
                    ♠ ♠ ♠ ♠
                    ♡ ♡
                    ◊ ◊
                    ♣ ♣ ♣ ♣ ♣

♠ ♠                ┌─────────┐              ♠ ♠ ♠
♡ ♡ ♡ ♡            │    N    │              ♡ ♡ ♡ ♡
◊ ◊ ◊ ◊ ◊          │ W     E │              ◊ ◊
♣ ♣                │    S    │              ♣ ♣ ♣ ♣
                   └─────────┘
                    ♠ ♠ ♠ ♠
                    ♡ ♡ ♡
                    ◊ ◊ ◊ ◊
                    ♣ ♣
```

b)

```
                    ♠
                    ♡ ♡
                    ◊ ◊ ◊ ◊ ◊ ◊
                    ♣ ♣ ♣ ♣

♠ ♠ ♠ ♠ ♠          ┌─────────┐              ♠ ♠ ♠ ♠
♡ ♡ ♡ ♡            │    N    │              ♡ ♡ ♡ ♡
◊                  │ W     E │              ◊ ◊
♣ ♣ ♣              │    S    │              ♣ ♣ ♣ ♣
                   └─────────┘
                    ♠ ♠ ♠
                    ♡ ♡ ♡
                    ◊ ◊ ◊ ◊
                    ♣ ♣ ♣
```

c)

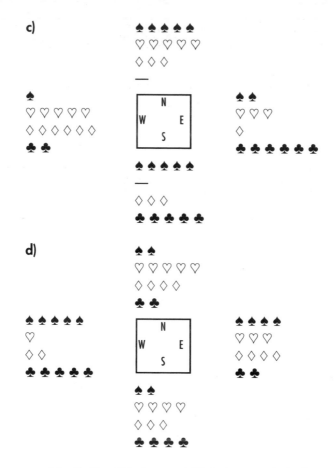

d)

2) Assume North-South's longest fit is ten cards in hearts, and East-West's longest fit is ten cards in spades. Which of the following are true?

   a) There should be 20 Total Tricks.

   b) If North-South have 24 high-card points, and East-West have only 16, then the LAW won't work.

   c) If North-South can make exactly four hearts, then East-West should be able to make four spades.

   d) If North-South have most of the high-cards and can make a small slam in hearts (12 tricks), then if East-West were to sacrifice in six spades they would be defeated four tricks.

3) If all four players have totally flat distribution (4-3-3-3 in some order), how many Total Tricks and Total Trumps should there be?

4) If East-West have an eight-card fit in clubs, diamonds, and hearts, then how many Total Tricks will be available on the full deal?

CHAPTER 1 ANSWERS

1) **a)** 8♠ + 8♡ = 16

    b) 10◇ + 9♠ = 19

    c) 10♠ + 8♡/♣ = 18

    d) 9♡ + 9♠ = 18

2) **a)** True. (10♡ + 10♠ = 20)

    b) False. The LAW works regardless of how the high-card points are divided.

    c) True. If there are 20 trumps, and one side can take ten tricks, then the other side can also take ten tricks.

    d) True. North-South have 12 tricks in hearts. East-West must have 20 (Total Tricks) minus 12 (North-South's tricks) equals eight tricks, or down four.

3) 7+7 = 14. If all hands are 4-3-3-3, then each side has a 4-3 fit in two suits.

4) 8+11 = 19. East-West have only 2 spades between them, so North-South must have 11 spades.

APPLYING THE LAW

CHAPTER 2

You've read the first chapter, and hopefully you're intrigued, if not surprised, by the LAW. But, perhaps you're saying, 'So what! Who cares if the Total Number of Trumps is equal to the Total Number of Tricks?' By the end of this chapter you'll start to see how vital the LAW is to making good competitive decisions at the table.

The key to using the LAW is to know how many trumps each side has. After the hand is played it's easy to know how many trumps each side held, and to see if the LAW worked. To know, during the auction, how many trumps there are is sometimes easy, but will often take some careful reasoning.

You usually have a fair idea of how many trumps your side has. If you're playing five-card majors, and you and your partner bid **1**♡ − **pass** − **2**♡, you probably have eight trumps.

If they open one heart, your partner overcalls one spade, and they raise to two hearts, you know a lot. They rate to have eight trumps and your partner will usually have five spades. If you are looking at four spades, you can conclude that there are probably 17 trumps (eight for them and nine for you).

This might seem too vague − too many 'probablys', and too much guessing. Just bear with it. Later on, especially in Chapter Four, we'll discover the many tools and inferences that make it easy to 'count the trumps' during the auction. Right now, we're just starting to think about how the LAW is helpful during the bidding.

Fortunately, to use the LAW effectively, we don't need an exact count of the trumps. We just need to be aware of how many trumps we think there are based on our own hand and the bidding.

We'll start with a simple example. Nobody's vulnerable and you hold

♠ K Q J 10 6 2   ♡ K Q 5   ◇ 4 3   ♣ 8 2

You open with one spade, and your left hand opponent (LHO) overcalls two diamonds; your partner raises to two spades and right hand opponent (RHO) bids three diamonds. The auction has gone:

You	LHO	Partner	RHO
1♠	2◇	2♠	3◇
??			

Most people play that bidding three spades here would be competitive — not invitational to game. Should we compete to three spades?

Let's think about how many trumps there are. Partner probably has three spades for his raise (and if he has four he'll probably go on to three spades no matter what we do), so our side has nine trumps. They have at least eight diamonds for their two-level overcall and raise — quite possibly nine — so the Total Number of Trumps is either 17 or 18.

Let's first look at what we should do if there are only 17 trumps (and therefore 17 Total Tricks). We'll have our answer by considering the chart below.

CHART FOR 17 TOTAL TRICKS Nobody Vulnerable			
We play the hand in three spades		They play the hand in three diamonds	
Our Tricks	Our Score	Their Tricks	Our Score
10	**+170**	7	+100
9	**+140**	8	+50
8	**−50**	9	−110
7	**−100**	10	−130

It will be important for the reader to understand this chart. The chart itself need not be memorized, but the reasoning we use to make such a chart is the essence of all Law of Total Tricks decisions.

From the bidding we have assumed that there are 17 trumps. The LAW tells us that we can expect 17 tricks. We want to consider how those 17 tricks can be divided, and what the resulting scores would be.

On the left half of the chart we see the results we'd get if we were to compete to three spades over their three diamonds. On the right side of the chart are the results if the opponents are allowed to play in three diamonds, i.e. we decide to pass.

As you can see, if we bid three spades and take ten tricks we'll score +170*. If we take nine tricks we'll score +140. If we take eight tricks we'll be -50, and if we have only seven tricks we'll be -100.

The next step is to see what would happen to the opponents in three diamonds in each of the corresponding cases.

If we can take ten tricks, they can take only seven, since we are expecting a total of 17. On the same line of the chart as our +170 for ten tricks is a score of +100, which we would receive if they played in three diamonds and took seven tricks. This tells us that, if the tricks are split ten for us and seven for them, we'd score better for playing the hand in three spades than we would for passing and defending against three diamonds.

Similarly, on the line where we score +140 for nine tricks is a corresponding score of +50, which we would receive if they took eight tricks in diamonds. Again, we score better for bidding three spades.

The last two lines of the chart show what happens if we are set in three spades, and the corresponding minus score we would get if the opponents played in three diamonds. Again, we achieve better scores for bidding three spades.

You will notice that, no matter how the 17 tricks are split, the scores on the left side of the chart (in boldface) always produce a better result than the right side. What does this tell us?

It tells us that we should compete to three spades over their three diamonds if we believe there are 17 trumps. We will expect 17 tricks, and no matter how they divide, we will score better for playing the hand in three spades than defending three diamonds.

But what if there are 18 trumps?

---

* All analyses in this book use duplicate scoring — see table in Appendix A.

CHART FOR 18 TOTAL TRICKS			
Nobody Vulnerable			
We play the hand in three spades		They play the hand in three diamonds	
Our Tricks	Our Score	Their Tricks	Our Score
10	+170	8	+50
9	+140	9	–110
8	–50	10	–130
7	–100	11	–150

Here, it's even more clear to bid on. The boldface scores are all on the left side of the chart. In particular, note the fact that each side might have nine tricks, and that bidding on produces a plus instead of a minus. With 18 trumps, no matter how the tricks are split, we will score better (left side of chart) in three spades than if we defend against three diamonds (right side of chart).

Here's what the full deal might look like with 18 trumps (in this example each side has nine tricks, for a total of 18 tricks):

```
                    ♠ A 5 4
                    ♡ A 10 4
                    ◇ 8 5
                    ♣ 10 6 5 4 3
    ♠ 9 7 3      ┌──────────┐      ♠ 8
    ♡ 9 7 2      │    N     │      ♡ J 8 6 3
    ◇ A K J 10 7 │ W     E  │      ◇ Q 9 6 2
    ♣ A Q        │    S     │      ♣ K J 9 7
                 └──────────┘
                    ♠ K Q J 10 6 2
                    ♡ K Q 5
                    ◇ 4 3
                    ♣ 8 2
```

Clearly then, if we think there are 18, or even 17 trumps, we want to bid three spades. The LAW explicitly tells us to. Granted, this might have been an easy problem to solve without the LAW, but the idea, for now, is to understand how thinking about the LAW can help you decide whether 'to bid or not to bid' in a competitive auction.

Let's say both sides are vulnerable and you hold:

♠ Q 10 5 4   ♡ Q 9 8 7 5   ◊ J 3 2   ♣ 7

Your partner opens a strong notrump and you bid Stayman, which gets doubled. You are pleased to hear partner bid two hearts, which you pass. Unfortunately the opponents balance with three clubs, which gets passed around to you. The bidding has gone:

Partner	RHO	You	LHO
1NT	pass	2♣	dbl
2♡	pass	pass	3♣
pass	pass	??	

In spite of your lack of high-card points, instinct tells you to bid three hearts, but let's see how we could use the LAW in this situation.

They probably have nine clubs (unless partner has four), and your side certainly has at least nine hearts, so the total number of trumps is quite likely to be 18. As we have already seen, with 18 trumps we want to out-bid them at the three-level. For practice, try running through the analysis (if we have n tricks then they have x tricks..., etc.). The LAW tells us to bid three hearts.

This is what the full deal might look like with 18 trumps and 18 tricks:

Both Vul.
South Dealer

```
                    ♠ Q 10 5 4
                    ♡ Q 9 8 7 5
                    ◊ J 3 2
                    ♣ 7
  ♠ 8 7 6 2              N              ♠ A 9
  ♡ 10 4          W           E         ♡ 6 3
  ◊ A 10 8 7            S              ◊ K 6 5
  ♣ A 9 3                              ♣ K Q 10 6 4 2
                    ♠ K J 3
                    ♡ A K J 2
                    ◊ Q 9 4
                    ♣ J 8 5
```

Here is one more simple example where the LAW might not be needed, but will certainly ensure that you know whether 'to bid or not to bid.' You are playing IMPs with both sides vulnerable and hold these cards:

♠ K 8 7 6   ♡ K 5 3   ◇ K 10 7 2   ♣ K J

You hear the following auction:

You	LHO	Partner	RHO
1◇	1♡	dbl	2♡
2♠	3♡	pass	pass
??			

You don't need to use your instincts, or try to guess what to do. This is a perfect situation for the Law of Total Tricks.

Your partner's negative double showed four spades, so your side has eight trumps. If your partner had a singleton heart, there is an excellent chance that he would have bid three spades over three hearts on his own. So partner rates to have a doubleton heart, and we can assume that the opponents have eight trumps.

We have eight and they have eight, for a total of 16 trumps and 16 tricks. Eventually, you will know off the top of your head what this tells you to do. For now, let's look at a chart for 16 trumps:

CHART FOR 16 TOTAL TRICKS			
Both Vulnerable			
We play the hand in three spades		They play the hand in three hearts	
Our Tricks	Our Score	Their Tricks	Our Score
10	+170	6	**+300**
9	+140	7	**+200**
8	–100	8	**+100**
7	–200	9	**–140**

As you can see, the right hand side (they play in three hearts) will produce a better score for us no matter how the tricks are divided. This means that we should pass and let them play in three hearts. Bidding on to three spades with only 16 trumps is not a winning proposition.

In particular, note the line where each side can take eight tricks. This happens to be the most likely occurrence when the points are fairly evenly divided between both sides, and there are only 16 trumps. In this scenario, neither partnership can make a three-level contract, and defending will produce +100, while bidding 'three-over-three' will result in -100.

With 16 trumps — eight per side, the full deal might be something like:

```
                    ♠ A Q 9 4
                    ♡ 8 4
                    ◇ Q J 5
                    ♣ 10 9 6 3
    ♠ J 10          ┌─────────┐        ♠ 5 3 2
    ♡ A 10 7 6 2    │    N    │        ♡ Q J 9
    ◇ 8 6 4         │ W     E │        ◇ A 9 3
    ♣ A Q 4         │    S    │        ♣ 8 7 5 2
                    └─────────┘
                    ♠ K 8 7 6
                    ♡ K 5 3
                    ◇ K 10 7 2
                    ♣ K J
```

Some competitive decisions are not as clear as the ones above. That's when it really helps to think about the LAW. Here's a deal where instinct alone might cost you a Spingold match.

In the early days with Marty Bergen, when I didn't fully understand the LAW, I held

♠ Q 8 3   ♡ K 10 4 2   ◇ 7 6 4   ♣ A 9 4,

with nobody vulnerable. Marty opened one club which was overcalled with a preemptive jump to two diamonds. I made a negative double (maybe not your choice, but certainly a possibility), LHO jumped preemptively to four diamonds, and Marty doubled. The auction so far:

LHO	Marty	RHO	Me
	1♣	2◇	dbl
4◇	dbl	pass	??

Should I pass the double or pull to four hearts?

First of all, partner's double is not 'penalty' — it just shows a good hand with a desire to compete. I know from my three little diamonds, and the opponents' bidding, that Marty must be short in diamonds. His most likely shapes are 4-4-1-4, 3-3-1-6, 3-4-1-5, and 4-3-1-5.

It feels as if the three small diamonds will fit very well — it's usually good to have nothing wasted opposite partner's short suit. This might make four hearts a good contract... *time-out*! This is a competitive auction — there's no need to worry about what fits with what — all we need to do is think about the LAW. It's relatively easy to use here.

Let's think about how many diamonds they're likely to have. Marty probably has one. If he were void, he would have been bidding a suit over four diamonds instead of doubling. He isn't likely to have a doubleton — the opponents' bidding suggests that they have more than an eight-card fit. So we can be pretty sure that Marty has exactly one diamond. Therefore, the opponents have nine trumps.

If we play the hand, it's probably going to be in hearts, and we rate to have eight of those. We might have only seven — but let's be generous for the time being. When doing this 'counting-the-trumps' process, we have to start somewhere. It's good practice always to start with a 'best-case' scenario, i.e. here we start out by assuming partner has four hearts. So, assume for the moment that they have nine diamonds and we have eight hearts. That makes seventeen Total Trumps, so there should be 17 tricks. Let's see in chart form what this means:

CHART FOR 17 TOTAL TRICKS Nobody Vulnerable			
We play the hand in four hearts		They play the hand in four diamonds doubled	
Our Tricks	Our Score	Their Tricks	Our Score
11	+450	6	**+800**
10	+420	7	**+500**
9	−50	8	**+300**
8	−100	9	**+100**

If we have an overtrick in four hearts (eleven tricks), then they'll be going down 800 (six tricks) in four diamonds doubled. If we make exactly four hearts (ten tricks), they will go down three (seven tricks) in four diamonds doubled. If we're going down one in four hearts (nine tricks), they're going down two in four diamonds doubled (eight tricks). And, even in the unlikely event that we're going down two in four hearts, we'll still beat them one in four diamonds. In all cases, we don't want to be on the left side of this chart — the side where bidding on always produces a smaller score than defending!

So, if we have eight trumps, and they have nine, it's clearly right to pass the double. No matter how the tricks are divided, we do better on defense — where all the bold-face scores are.

What if we have only seven trumps? That makes pass even more clear. (You can go through the math yourself — assume 16 Total Tricks and see what the LAW says about passing versus bidding on.)

Remember how we assumed the best-case scenario? We 'gave' partner four hearts. You might have been uncomfortable with that, but all we really needed was a starting point. You can see now that, whether we give him four hearts or three hearts, it doesn't really matter. In either case, the LAW screams 'pass.'

Sometimes you'll reach one conclusion with the LAW if partner has three hearts, and a different one if he has four hearts. In that case you might just have to use your judgment. Fortunately, in this example it made no difference whether he had three or four. At the table I ignored the LAW and used my instincts, which told me to bid four hearts. This was the full deal:

```
                        ♠ A J 5 2
                        ♡ A 8 7 5
                        ◇ 3
                        ♣ K Q J 5
    ♠ 10 9 7 6        ┌─────────┐        ♠ K 4
    ♡ Q J 9 3         │    N    │        ♡ 6
    ◇ A K 8           │ W     E │        ◇ Q J 10 9 5 2
    ♣ 8 7             │    S    │        ♣ 10 6 3 2
                      └─────────┘
                        ♠ Q 8 3
                        ♡ K 10 4 2
                        ◇ 7 6 4
                        ♣ A 9 4
```

We lost a spade, two hearts and a diamond, and went one down in four hearts, -50. East-West would have lost one spade, one heart and at least two clubs. Assuming a trump lead (the correct lead) they'd lose at least three clubs and could easily be held to eight (possibly even seven) tricks. Not surprisingly, North-South had nine tricks and East-West had eight, for a total of 17 tricks — to match the 17 trumps.

You might think it was unlucky that hearts broke 4-1. Not so. If they had split 3-2 that would simply translate into four diamonds doubled going down an extra trick, still making 'pass' the winner. That's the point of the LAW. *There are only so many tricks available on a deal* (dictated by the total number of trumps). If the opponents' suits split 3-2 when you play the hand, they still split 3-2 if the opponents play the hand. That's going to translate into extra losers for the opponents if they buy the contract. The 4-1 heart break cost me a trick in four hearts — but it would have added a trick to East-West's four diamond contract since they would have had only one heart loser instead of two. It's the same concept as moving a finesse onside for us, which makes it offside for them. You can move cards wherever you like, but I still should have realized that there were simply not enough trumps (or tricks) to warrant bidding on. If I had used the LAW we would have won the match — we ended up losing by 5 IMPs*!

We must give Marty credit for his double of four diamonds. Most players holding the North hand would blindly guess to bid four-of-a-major and play in a seven or eight-card fit. Double was a much better action, since it allowed partner to leave it in if he had some diamond length (in this case a tripleton), and nothing special in the way of major-suit length. West's four-diamond bid was questionable, but it certainly worked well when I didn't obey the LAW.

Let's look now at the first World Championship decision from Chapter One. You're South, holding

♠ A K Q 8 6   ♡ 10 7 6 3   ◇ J 8   ♣ A 10

with nobody vulnerable, and you're on your way to winning the 1978 World Pairs Championship in New Orleans. Your one-spade opening is overcalled with two hearts and, after your

---

* IMP scoring is used for all "Team" matches in this book — see Appendix B.

partner raises to two spades, your RHO jumps to four hearts. Should you pass, double or bid four spades?

Neither Vul.
Dealer South

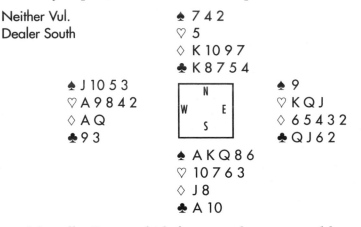

```
                      ♠ 7 4 2
                      ♡ 5
                      ◇ K 10 9 7
                      ♣ K 8 7 5 4
  ♠ J 10 5 3           N            ♠ 9
  ♡ A 9 8 4 2    W           E      ♡ K Q J
  ◇ A Q               S            ◇ 6 5 4 3 2
  ♣ 9 3                            ♣ Q J 6 2
                      ♠ A K Q 8 6
                      ♡ 10 7 6 3
                      ◇ J 8
                      ♣ A 10
```

Marcello Branco bid four spades, as would many top players who neglect the LAW, found himself doubled, and should have been defeated. West led the ace of hearts and shifted to the ace and queen of diamonds. Branco crossed to the ace of clubs and ruffed a heart in dummy. He now pitched a heart on the ten of diamonds, as West ruffed in for the defense's third trick, leaving:

```
                      ♠ 7 4
                      ♡ —
                      ◇ 9
                      ♣ K 8 7 5
  ♠ J 10 5             N            ♠ 9
  ♡ 9 8 4        W           E      ♡ J
  ◇ —                 S            ◇ 6 5
  ♣ 3                              ♣ Q J 6
                      ♠ A K Q 8 6
                      ♡ 10
                      ◇ —
                      ♣ 10
```

If West had returned a club declarer would have lost another trick for down one. But, this was Branco's lucky day — West played a heart, and Branco was +590*.

---

* Branco could have made the hand on a double-dummy basis after the first three tricks.

Branco shouldn't have had to rely on luck. He could have used the LAW and doubled four hearts instead of bidding four spades. He could have expected from the bidding that his partner had three spades and one heart (with four spades or no hearts his partner would bid four spades on his own), and that there would be only eight trumps for each side. This meant that there were 8+8, or 16 Total Trumps, and Tricks. If four spades was making (+420, ten tricks), then four hearts doubled would be down four (+700 — old scoring, six tricks). The LAW would have told him to double, and the penalty he would have collected wouldn't have stopped him from winning the event!

Let's look at a different decision. With nobody vulnerable, your LHO opens the bidding with five clubs which your partner doubles. Your RHO passes and you are looking at

♠ A 4 3   ♡ Q J 10 5 4   ◇ 9 6 3   ♣ 8 2

Perhaps you think this is easy — maybe your instincts tell you what to do.

All we really have to do, though, is think about the LAW. We don't *know* how many Total Trumps there are, but we don't need to. We start by making assumptions, and usually that will lead us to an easy solution.

The five-club bidder probably has an eight-card suit, and you have two, which leaves three clubs between RHO and your partner. Let's assume partner has one club. Yes, he *might* have a void, or a doubleton, or maybe even three, but we have to start somewhere.

Partner probably has at least one four-card major, and there is a good chance that, by bidding five hearts, we will wind up in a nine-card fit. In fact, let's see what would happen if partner had 4-4-4-1 distribution. That would mean that we have nine hearts and they have ten clubs, for a total of 19 tricks.

CHART FOR 19 TOTAL TRICKS
Nobody Vulnerable

We play the hand in five hearts		They play the hand in five clubs doubled	
Our Tricks	**Our Score**	**Their Tricks**	**Our Score**
12	+480*	7	**+800**
11	+450	8	**+500**
10	-50	9	**+300**
9	-100	10	**+100**

* **Bidding and making a slam (+980) is a rare occurence in competitive auctions, and shouldn't factor into our decision.**

As you can see, bidding on cannot be the winning action. The 'We play the hand' side always produces a smaller score than the 'They play the hand' side.

All we have to do is think about 4-4-4-1, and we know what to do. If there are 19 trumps, 'pass' is a standout. If there are fewer than 19 trumps, 'pass' will stand out even more. What if partner happened to be 4-4-3-2, resulting in nine hearts and nine clubs, for only 18 trumps?

Try to fill in the blanks of the following chart. You can probably do it in your head; while you do so, take note of the difference between defending or bidding five hearts on a line by line basis:

CHART FOR 18 TOTAL TRICKS
Nobody Vulnerable

We play the hand in five hearts		They play the hand in five clubs doubled	
Our Tricks	**Our Score**	**Their Tricks**	**Our Score**
12	—	—	—
11	—	—	—
10	—	—	—
9	—	—	—

Were there any situations where bidding five-of-a-major produced a better result than defending five clubs doubled?

Even if there are 20 trumps, bidding five-of-a-major would only be right if we have exactly 11 tricks (+450) leaving them with exactly nine tricks (+300). For there to be 20 trumps, we'd need partner to have *four*-card heart support and a club void, or to have *five*-card heart support — not very likely possibilities.

By now, I hope you can see how trivial it is to pass if you think about the LAW. You didn't even need to know the exact number of trumps. We started with an assumption, 'what if partner has one club... and what if we have nine trumps...' We then found out that, if there were 19 trumps, we should pass. With that as a starting point we were able to figure out what to do if there were more or fewer than 19 trumps.

Let's now try the second World Championship decision presented in Chapter One. You were in the seat of Gabino Cintra, holding

♠ A Q 7 6 2   ♡ A   ◇ A 7 6 3   ♣ 10 9 6

vulnerable against not. You opened the bidding one spade and faced the following decision:

West	North	East	South
Rodrigue	*Branco*	*Priday*	*You*
		pass	1♠
2♣	2♡	3♣	3◇
4♣	4♠	5♣	??

Cintra, like most experts unfamiliar with the LAW, made the most common error of competitive bidding. He presumably decided that, because of his ♣109x, his partner was short in clubs. Therefore the hands 'fit well' and, accordingly, he bid on to five spades.

What would the LAW have told him? He'd first have had to estimate partner's expected black-suit length. From the bidding it was likely that his partner had a singleton club, and three-card spade support. That would mean nine clubs for the opponents and eight spades for his side, for a total of 17 trumps and 17 tricks.

If he could take eleven tricks in his five-spade contract, that would translate into six tricks for the opponents in their five-club contract — a nice penalty (+900 in those days, +1100 with today's scoring!). If he were to make fewer than eleven tricks in five spades, of course, he should still double five clubs. This was the full deal:

N-S Vul.
Dealer East

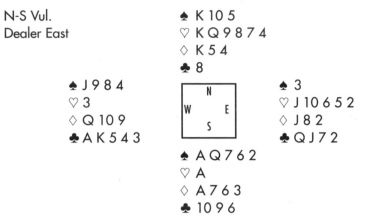

    ♠ K 10 5
    ♡ K Q 9 8 7 4
    ◇ K 5 4
    ♣ 8

♠ J 9 8 4   ♠ 3
♡ 3   ♡ J 10 6 5 2
◇ Q 10 9   ◇ J 8 2
♣ A K 5 4 3   ♣ Q J 7 2

    ♠ A Q 7 6 2
    ♡ A
    ◇ A 7 6 3
    ♣ 10 9 6

Cintra might have made five spades if he could have seen through the backs of the cards, but, not unnaturally, he was defeated one trick for -100. Repeated trump leads would hold five clubs doubled to seven tricks! No student of the LAW should be surprised that there were ten tricks taken in spades, and that there would have been only seven tricks available in clubs — for a total of 17.

Cintra could have assumed from the bidding that there were only 17 trumps (and tricks), in which case he would have doubled five clubs instead of bidding on to the doomed five spades. Even if you're not yet convinced to double five clubs, perhaps you can see that, at the very least, he could have made a forcing pass and left it up to his partner.

The next two decisions we'll discuss are related to the kind of auction that will come up nearly every session. They're the sort of decisions one needs to get right to be a consistent winner. We're going to look at the auction first from responder's point of view, then we'll switch seats and look at opener's problem.

From responder's point of view:

Opener	RHO	Responder	LHO
1♠	2♡	2♠	3♡
pass	pass	??	

With both vulnerable at IMPs, this is responder's hand:

♠ J 8 3 2   ♡ 6   ◊ K J 5 2   ♣ Q 8 6 4

Despite his minimum in high-cards, instinct tells him to bid three spades — and so does the LAW. He knows that his side has nine trumps, and that the opponents probably have eight or nine.

Using the LAW, his first step is to think, 'What if they have nine?' There would be 18 Total Trumps — and 18 Total Tricks. We saw earlier that we should always bid three-over-three if there are 18 trumps. Now we consider, 'What if they have eight hearts, so that there are only 17 trumps?' We also examined this possibility earlier. We saw that with 17 trumps, one side rates to make their three-level contract, while the other side is going down only one. That led us to the conclusion that it's still okay to outbid the opponents at the three-level, if there are 17 trumps.

Of course, if responder had to guess which was more likely, he'd guess that there were 18 trumps (he's looking at only one heart — for them to have only eight trumps would mean that his partner has four hearts). So, looking at four spades and one heart, responder will certainly compete to three spades over three hearts.

Now, let's walk over to opener's seat.

Opener	LHO	Responder	RHO
1♠	2♡	2♠	3♡
??			

Opener is looking at:

♠ K Q 10 7 4   ♡ K 5 2   ◊ A Q 4   ♣ 10 9

He has 5-3-3-2 distribution and is trying to decide what to do over their three-heart bid. Should he bid three spades or pass the decision to his partner? We have just seen that if he passes, his partner will compete to three spades if he's looking at four spades and one heart, because he'll assume that there are 18 trumps. Even if responder is holding four spades and two hearts, he'll assume that there are 17 trumps (nine spades and eight hearts), and still bid on. Responder could even bid three spades holding three spades and one heart — again assuming 17 trumps (eight spades and nine hearts). So, opener doesn't need to think in terms of partner having four spades or a singleton heart, since with those holdings he will compete to three spades on his own.

Now we can start to 'count' the trumps in order to make our own decision. We have eight (remember, if we have nine, partner will know what to do). They have eight (again, if they have nine, partner will have only one and will know to bid on). From our point of view, then, the total is 16 trumps, or 16 tricks. What does this tell us? Earlier we saw in chart form that with 16 trumps we should not outbid the opponents at the three-level. The most likely scenario is that both sides will have only eight tricks, and bidding will turn a plus into a minus. This tells us to pass the three-heart bid and leave it up to partner.

The Law of Total Tricks logic (look again at the charts) leads us to state as an absolute rule:

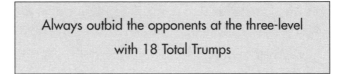

> Never outbid the opponents at the three-level
> with 16 Total Trumps

We already saw that we should:

> Always outbid the opponents at the three-level
> with 18 Total Trumps

With 17 Total Trumps it is usually right to outbid them on the three-level. Of course, you should consider the vulnerability and the form of scoring, but the rules for 16 and 18 trumps are pretty good ones to follow blindly!

Now let's return to Rio de Janeiro and the third World Championship deal from Chapter One. Mike Passell could have blindly followed the 'Rule of 16' if he had known about it, as you do now! Recall that he held

♠ J 9 3   ♡ Q 8 6   ◊ A 7 4 3   ♣ A 5 3,

at favorable vulnerability, and faced this decision:

West	North	East	South
Passell	Belladonna	Brachman	Pittala
	1◊	1♡	1♠
2♡	3♣	pass	pass
??			

Yes, he might have cuebid two diamonds on the first round, but he'd still be facing essentially the same decision. His partner almost certainly has only five hearts (with six he'd bid to the three-level himself). It's conceivable that the opponents have nine clubs, but quite unlikely. If you had to guess, you'd assume that they have at most an eight-card fit, since partner will often bid three hearts holding a singleton club.

This is the typical eight-and-eight situation that comes up all the time. The strength is evenly divided between North-South and East-West, and both sides have eight trumps. Once one side gets to the three-level, it doesn't pay to bid on. If the 16 tricks are split eight-and-eight (as they often are), then bidding will turn a plus into a minus! Neither side can make a three-level contract.

You can, if you wish, make up your own chart to see what happens when you bid three-over-three with only 16 trumps, or you can go through the analysis in your head. Don't be influenced by a high-card maximum or minimum. Just base your decision on how many trumps there are, and remember that 16 trumps are not enough to bid three-over-three. No matter which way you do it, be sure to think about the Law of Total Tricks when faced with the kind of decision Mike Passell met in the World Championships.

Passell, perhaps influenced by his extra high-card points, bid on to three hearts which ended the auction. On the actual deal there weren't even 16 trumps:

N-S Vul.
Dealer North

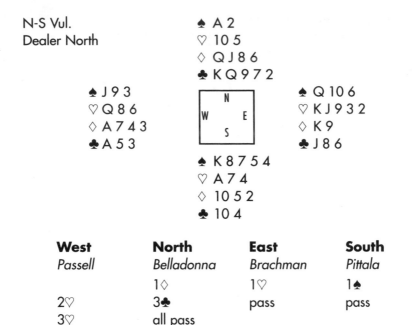

```
                        ♠ A 2
                        ♡ 10 5
                        ◇ Q J 8 6
                        ♣ K Q 9 7 2
      ♠ J 9 3            ┌─────────┐        ♠ Q 10 6
      ♡ Q 8 6            │    N    │        ♡ K J 9 3 2
      ◇ A 7 4 3         W│         │E        ◇ K 9
      ♣ A 5 3            │    S    │        ♣ J 8 6
                        └─────────┘
                        ♠ K 8 7 5 4
                        ♡ A 7 4
                        ◇ 10 5 2
                        ♣ 10 4
```

West	North	East	South
Passell	*Belladonna*	*Brachman*	*Pittala*
	1◇	1♡	1♠
2♡	3♣	pass	pass
3♡	all pass		

Brachman was held to seven tricks in three hearts (-100) instead of the +100 that could have been recorded against three clubs. Even if North-South had had one more club, there still would not have been enough trumps to bid three-over-three. This decision 'only' cost the U.S.A. team 5 IMPs, and in fact they went on to win the World Championship. But this is the kind of decision that comes up day after day, and costs good players 5 IMPs time after time.

A similar decision came up in an Allendale, New Jersey sectional when Lisa Berkowitz, many times a national champion, held

♠ Q 3 ♡ 10 8 3 2 ◇ A K Q 4 ♣ A 6 2

and heard her partner open a weak two spades as the dealer in a pairs game. Her side was not vulnerable, and her vulnerable opponent overcalled three hearts. Lisa and her partner were playing the modern style where a weak two-bid (especially at this vulnerability) could be based on a five-card suit. Despite this, she chose to bid three spades, which means that she ignored the LAW!

Even if her partner had held a six-card spade suit, her side would have had only eight trumps. Her partner was unlikely to be void in hearts — a singleton or doubleton is what might be expected. If her partner held only one heart that would mean that there were eight trumps for the opponents. Eight for them, eight for us, making 16. We have already seen that we shouldn't bid three-over-three with 16. Just think — if her partner held only five spades, or as many as two or three hearts, then there would be only 15 or even 14 trumps. If there are fewer than 16 trumps, then it would be that much more wrong to bid three-over-three.

This violation of the 'Rule of 16' is committed by players of all-levels, every day. Here's one from the 1984 World Team Olympiad in Seattle, where both Easts in the team match committed the kind of error that readers of this book will no longer make. They held

♠ Q 6 2   ♡ Q 6 5   ◊ K Q 6 5   ♣ 9 8 7

with neither vulnerable, and heard this typical auction:

West	North	East	South
1♠	2♣	2♠	3♣
pass	pass	??	

They looked at their three small clubs and their maximum, and decided that they had good reason to bid three spades. Their partner was 5-3-3-2 and took eight tricks. Three clubs would also have taken eight tricks. Both went -50 instead of +50. Not really a terrible disaster, but by now you realize that this kind of decision, which comes up frequently, should become much easier for you at the table. You'll be winning 3 IMPs here and 5 IMPs there, and those IMPs will add up in a hurry.

You can use the Law of Total Tricks in all kinds of competitive bidding decisions. Here is a mildly eccentric problem that appeared in Britain's *International Popular Bridge Monthly*. With North-South vulnerable, the South player held:

♠ 6 4 2   ♡ K Q J 10 6 4   ◊ A 4   ♣ A J

and his RHO opened the bidding with three hearts! This was the unusual auction:

West	North	East	South
		3♡!	pass
pass	dbl	pass	pass
4♣	pass	pass	??

This was posed as a hypothetical problem to a panel of experts. Most of them concluded that partner must have a heart void, and from the failure to double four clubs, probably only three cards there. It followed that North's most likely distribution was 5-0-5-3. Good logic so far. Now, this becomes an easy Law of Total Tricks decision, but the panelists failed to see it.

If we use the good assumption that partner is 5-0-5-3, and add that to our 3-6-2-2, we know how many trumps there are. The opponents have eight clubs, and we have eight spades. There are going to be 16 tricks on this deal.

Many of the panelists voted to bid four spades, which can't possibly be right. If four spades is making (ten tricks), then what is happening to four clubs doubled? If we have ten tricks, they have only six! Would we rather be +620 or +800? Not a big deal, but what about some of the other ways the 16 tricks could be split? Try running through a 'chart analysis' in your head. You'll see that no matter how the 16 tricks are divided, it will always be right to double four clubs!

Although the full deal was not given, it is more than likely that the 16 tricks are split something like eight-and-eight, or nine-and-seven, making double a big winner. Using the LAW on deals like this can easily turn a problem into a non-problem.

Let's take a look at the last World Championship hand from Chapter One, where Italy faced North America in the Bermuda Bowl final.

You were partnered by the great Giorgio Belladonna and held the following cards:

♠ K 9 7 3 2   ♡ 9 4   ◇ A Q 10   ♣ J 8 2

Vulnerable against not you faced the following decision:

West	North	East	South
Goldman	Belladonna	Soloway	You
		pass	pass
1♣	1◇	2♡	2♠
3♡	pass	pass	??

At the table, Vito Pittala bid four diamonds. Does the LAW suggest that he did the right thing? He could expect that his side had eight diamonds, and that the opponents had eight or nine hearts, for a total of 16 or 17 trumps.

You can look back at the charts if you wish, or you can reason as follows: 'There are 16 or 17 trumps. If I bid four diamonds and make it (ten tricks), then the opponents were only going to take six or seven tricks in three hearts. So, bidding four diamonds might get us a score of +130 instead of +100 or +150 on defense. If I bid four diamonds and am defeated (we take nine tricks), then the opponents were going to take seven or eight tricks in three hearts. So, bidding four diamonds might get us a score of -100 instead of +50 or +100. If four diamonds is defeated two tricks for -200 (we take eight tricks — they take eight or nine), I will turn +50 or -140 into -200.'

Clearly, the LAW should have warned Pittala against bidding four diamonds. This was the full deal:

```
N-S Vul.                    ♠ 10 8
Dealer East                 ♡ K J 7
                            ◇ K 9 7 5 3
                            ♣ A Q 9
        ♠ A J 4          ┌──────────┐     ♠ Q 6 5
        ♡ A 8 3          │    N     │     ♡ Q 10 6 5 2
        ◇ J 2            │ W     E  │     ◇ 8 6 4
        ♣ K 10 6 4 3     │    S     │     ♣ 7 5
                         └──────────┘
                            ♠ K 9 7 3 2
                            ♡ 9 4
                            ◇ A Q 10
                            ♣ J 8 2
```

Belladonna was defeated after Soloway's club lead. If he drew trumps he'd end up with two heart losers — so he tried to set up spades before drawing trumps. The defense continued clubs and eventually held declarer to nine tricks. It looks like three hearts would have been held to seven tricks for the expected 16 Trick Total. There simply were not enough trumps to be at the four-level!

The hands presented in this chapter are just a tiny sampling of the infinite number of deals where a good working knowledge of the LAW will vastly improve your game. Try not to be bothered by all of the charts and the lengthy mathematical analyses. As you read some of the later chapters in the book, you will acquire some general rules and maxims that will make using the LAW at the table much easier. The next chapter gets into a few finer points so that it will be easier for you to analyze deals in the later chapters from a Law of Total Tricks point of view.

CHAPTER REVIEW

- The key to using the LAW during the bidding is to know how many trumps each side has.

- An exact count on the number of trumps is not always easy — but an approximation is all that is necessary.

- Before making any competitive bidding decision, the first step is to make a mental count of how many trumps each side rates to have, based on the previous bidding.

- The second step, after 'counting the trumps,' is to go through a 'chart analysis.' Say to yourself, 'I'm assuming 18 trumps... if they are making x number of tricks, then their score would be y... so, if I bid on, it would mean that we're making n number of tricks, and our score would be z.'

- When in doubt about the number of trumps, start out with either a 'worst-case scenario' or a 'best-case scenario.'

- With 18 or more Total Trumps you should always bid three-over-three.

- With 16 or fewer Total Trumps you should never bid three-over-three.

- As you gain experience with the LAW, it will become easier to make deductions about how many trumps each side has.

- Fine-tuning of the LAW will be introduced in the next chapter.

1) You conclude from the competitive auction that there are 17 trumps. You think the opponents have eight hearts and your side has nine spades. They have bid up to three hearts and nobody is vulnerable.

   a) Fill in the blanks in the following chart:

CHART FOR 17 TOTAL TRICKS Nobody Vulnerable			
We play the hand in three spades		They play the hand in three hearts	
Our Tricks	Our Score	Their Tricks	Our Score
10	—	—	—
9	—	—	—
8	—	—	—
7	—	—	—

   b) What does the chart suggest you do over three hearts?

2) Your hand is

   ♠ A K 8 5 3   ♡ 9 7   ◊ Q 6 5 4   ♣ 7 2

   On each of the following auctions try to estimate the total number of trumps/tricks (assume five-card majors).

   a)

LHO	Partner	RHO	You
1♡	1♠	2♡	??

   b)

LHO	Partner	RHO	You
1♡	dbl	3♡	??

   c)

LHO	Partner	RHO	You
1◊	pass	1♡	1♠
2♡	2♠	pass	??

d)	**LHO**	**Partner**	**RHO**	**You**
	3♡	dbl	4♡	??

e)	**LHO**	**Partner**	**RHO**	**You**
	3♣	dbl	5♣	??

3) For each of the problems in Question 2, assume nobody is vulnerable. What does the LAW suggest you do in each case?

4) Is there any competitive situation in which you should ignore or not use the LAW?

5) Will the LAW always work out exactly?

6) All of the following bidding problems can be solved by using the 'chart logic' and other information presented thus far. Assume you are playing in a Team-of-Four Match with nobody vulnerable. Do the best you can at estimating how many trumps everybody has — it will get easier with time and a little bit of practice.

a)	**LHO**	**Partner**	**RHO**	**You**
		2♡	3♣	??

♠ A 8 5 3   ♡ Q 7   ◇ Q 10 3   ♣ K 8 3 2

b)	**LHO**	**Partner**	**RHO**	**You**
				1♠
	2♣	2♠	3♣	??

♠ K J 7 6 5   ♡ A J 4   ◇ A 9   ♣ J 7 6

c)	**LHO**	**Partner**	**RHO**	**You**
		1♡	1♠	2♡
	2♠	pass	pass	??

♠ 9 7   ♡ Q 8 6 4   ◇ K 10 8 3   ♣ 7 3 2

d)	**LHO**	**Partner**	**RHO**	**You**
	1♡	1♠	2♡	2♠
	3♡	pass	pass	??

♠ Q 10 3 2   ♡ 4   ◇ K Q 7 5   ♣ 8 7 6 2

e)

LHO	Partner	RHO	You
1♣	dbl	4♣	??

♠ A 10 5 3 ♡ A 3 2 ◇ Q 6 5 ♣ K 7 5

f)

LHO	Partner	RHO	You
pass	1♠	pass	pass
2♣	2♡	3♣	??

♠ 10 9 7 4 ♡ 7 4 ◇ 8 6 5 4 3 ♣ 3 2

g)

LHO	Partner	RHO	You
1♣	2♠	4♡	??

♠ A 8 ♡ 9 7 6 ◇ A 9 5 3 ♣ 8 7 3 2

h)

LHO	Partner	RHO	You
			1♠
dbl	3♠¹	4♡	??

1. Preemptive.

♠ A K Q J 5 ♡ K J 8 2 ◇ J 7 ♣ K 5

i)

LHO	Partner	RHO	You
			1◇
1♡	2◇	2♡	??

♠ K 4 ♡ A 9 7 ◇ Q 10 9 7 5 ♣ K 8 6

j)

LHO	Partner	RHO	You
			1◇
pass	1♠	pass	2♠
pass	pass	3♡	??

♠ 10 6 4 2 ♡ 8 ◇ A J 6 3 ♣ A K 7 5

1) **a)**

CHART FOR 17 TOTAL TRICKS			
Nobody Vulnerable			
We play the hand in three spades		They play the hand in three hearts	
Our Tricks	Our Score	Their Tricks	Our Score
10	**+170**	7	+100
9	**+140**	8	+ 50
8	**−50**	9	−140
7	**−100**	10	−170

b) Bid three spades. The only time this will be wrong is if one side had only seven tricks and double was a possibility.

2) **a)** 18 (eight for them, ten for you)

b) 18 (nine for them, nine for you)

c) 16 (eight for them, eight for you)

d) 18 or 19 (nine or ten for them, nine for you)

e) 17, 18, or 19 (nine or ten for them, eight or nine for you)

3) **a)** Bid four spades (only wrong if each side has exactly nine tricks). Waiting to see what they do is acceptable, but the direct jump is preferable.

b) Bid four spades (this will be wrong only if each side has exactly nine tricks). Bidding only three spades is possible.

c) Pass, for now. If they compete to three hearts, let them play there. Partner will go on to three spades over three hearts if he has four card support.

d) Bid four spades. This will only be wrong if each side had nine tricks.

e) Double. If we can make five spades, they should be going down four. Think of the 'chart.'

4) No. Always try to use the LAW in competitive auctions. It is more accurate than even the best player's judgment.

5) No. However, after reading Chapter Three you'll be able to achieve much greater accuracy.

6) **a)** Pass. Your side has at most eight hearts, and they have at most eight clubs (barring the remote chance that partner is void!). With a maximum of 16 Total Trumps, don't bid three-over-three!

b) Pass. Again we expect 16 trumps, and should pass. For there to be more than 16 trumps partner would have to have either a fourth spade, or a singleton club — and in both cases he would know to bid three spades by himself.

c) Three hearts. Don't be influenced by your lack of high-card points. There are at least 17 trumps (eight for them and nine for us), and if you go through the 'chart analysis,' you'll see that you shouldn't pass.

d) Three spades. In spite of your high-card minimum, the LAW says that you should bid, since there are quite likely to be 18 trumps.

e) Double. Most people play this as 'responsive.' Even if you play it as pure 'penalty,' you should still double. Opposite 4-4-4-1 there are eight spades and nine clubs for only 17 trumps and 17 tricks. The 'chart' shows that it would be wrong to bid four spades.

f) Three spades. Yes, you have a zero count — but what does the LAW say? We have at least nine trumps, and the opponents have at least eight, for a total of 17 or more. We don't want to let them play in three clubs, since we know that at least one partnership can take nine tricks.

g) Pass. There is no indication that there are enough Total Trumps to warrant any other action.

h) Double (or pass). Partner rates to have four spades and one heart — for a Total of only 17 trumps. Why should we contract for 10 tricks?

i) Three diamonds. You have nine, they have at least eight. This might seem easy, but the player facing this decision in the 1985 Bermuda Bowl passed and lost a partscore swing.

j) Three spades. Either they can make three hearts, or you can make three spades! There have to be at least 17 tricks (ensuring nine for one side). Partner can't be 4-4 in the majors (he would have responded one heart), so he either has five spades (giving your side nine), or he has only three hearts (giving their side nine.)

MINOR
ADJUSTMENTS

CHAPTER 3

As we have already seen, the LAW does not work out exactly on every hand. In fact, without knowing how to 'adjust' the LAW, you will find that it is frequently 'off' by a trick. 'Adjusting' is not a gimmick to make the LAW work. It is a natural process with its own set of rules. So that you understand better why it is necessary to adjust, let's talk for a moment about how players are first taught to bid.

We learn in the beginning that an ace counts as four points, a king three, a queen two, and a jack one. We add up the pictures and come up with our high-card points. In a similar manner, we have seen in the first two chapters how to count up the number of trumps and the number of tricks for any given deal. When we learn to bid, it isn't long before we're taught about distribution, and the value of spot-cards. In order to better evaluate a hand for bidding, we learn to add points for singletons or voids, or for long suits. We're shown that:

♠ Q 10 9 8 ♡ K J 9 8 ◊ J 10 ♣ A 10 9

is a better hand than:

♠ Q 5 3 2 ♡ K J 6 3 ◊ J 2 ♣ A 6 5

We also discover that it's good to have points in our long suits, so that:

♠ A K Q 8 7 ♡ K 8 7 6 ◊ 8 7 6 ♣ 6

is a better hand than:

♠ 8 7 6 5 4 ♡ 8 7 6 5 ◊ A K Q ♣ K

We learn to open the bidding with:

♠ A 8 7 6 5 ♡ A Q 8 7 5 ◊ 9 8 3 ♣ —

but to pass with:

♠ A 8 7 6 ♡ A 8 7 ◊ 9 8 3 ♣ Q 8 3

Similarly, as far as the Law of Total Tricks is concerned, we need to be aware that holdings like QJx and K10x in the opponents' suits are different from xxx and Axx. The 'soft' holdings of QJx and K10x will almost always produce a trick for us on defense, if that suit is trumps. However, if we play the hand in our own trump suit, our holding of QJx or K10x in the opponents' suit will often prove to be worthless. For example, what happens when partner has a small doubleton in their trump suit opposite our QJx? Let's say that this is the full deal:

```
            ♠ A 6 4 3
            ♡ 8 5
            ◇ Q 9 7 2
            ♣ Q 6 4
♠ 9 8 2        ┌─────────┐        ♠ 10 5
♡ A 10 7 4     │    N    │        ♡ K 9 6 3
◇ 10 6 5       │ W     E │        ◇ A K 8 3
♣ A 7 2        │    S    │        ♣ 9 8 5
               └─────────┘
            ♠ K Q J 7
            ♡ Q J 2
            ◇ J 4
            ♣ K J 10 3
```

Each side has eight trumps — but there are not 16 Total Tricks. North-South have eight tricks in spades (losing two hearts, two diamonds, and a club), but East-West have only seven tricks in hearts. In addition to their five side-suit losers, East-West must lose a trump trick. That holding of QJx of hearts is useless to North-South in their spade contract, but it's worth a full trick on defense.

Similarly, a holding of K10x is often worth a trick on defense, but not on offense. What if the suit is laid out as follows:

```
                 K 10 x
               ┌─────────┐
Q J x x        │    N    │        A x x x
               │ W     E │
               │    S    │
               └─────────┘
                  x x
```

Clearly, East-West must lose a trick in this trump suit. Meanwhile, if North-South play the hand in their own trump suit, they are unlikely to benefit from the fact that the ten can eventually be set up as a trick.

What does this mean as far as the LAW is concerned? It means that when you have 'soft' holdings (such as QJx — a complete list can be found in Chapter Nine) in the opponents' suits, you should consider making a downward adjustment to the trick count. An ace will take a trick no matter which side plays the hand, but a holding of QJx will be a useful trick only about half of the time (the half when you are on defense).

There are also factors which suggest adding to the trick count. Very 'pure' trump suits of your own such as QJ10xx opposite AKxx, with no wasted queens and jacks in the side suits, will often produce extra tricks. Also, if both sides have a big double-fit with good shape, there tend to be extra tricks. This next deal illustrates these positive adjustment factors.

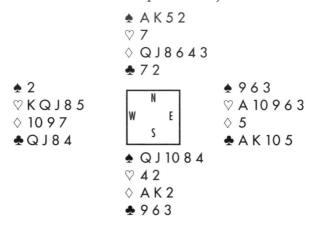

Here, the big fit, along with the pure suits, yields 21 tricks, even though there are only 19 trumps.

As you analyze the LAW at work on many deals, you'll find that it is frequently 'off' by a trick or two. This phenomenon is almost always attributable to pure or unpure holdings in each side's trump suit (or one of several other 'adjustment factors').

> When deciding how many trumps (tricks) there are
> on a deal, 'soft' holdings in the opponents' suits
> should cause you to lower your estimate of the Total
> Trick count. Therefore, if you're not sure whether to
> bid on or defend, you'll be more inclined to defend
> when you have these holdings.

All of the ideas just laid out are explained in more detail in Chapter Nine. There's no need for a long technical barrage at this point, but if you feel scientific, you can read Chapter Nine now, and return to this point as opposed to reading it in sequence.

CHAPTER REVIEW

- When using the Law of Total Tricks, it is helpful to be aware of the need for 'adjustments.'

- Negative adjustments usually result from soft holdings in the opponents' trump suit and should cause you to lower your estimate of the Total Number of Tricks.

- Pure hands and super fits with wild distribution cause a positive adjustment to the trick count.

- A more complete explanation of this subject can be found in Chapter Nine. (Scientific, or curious, readers can read Chapter Nine at this time.)

ON THE PROPER LEVEL

CHAPTER 4

You're opposing the world's most successful pair for many years, Bob Hamman and Bobby Wolff, in the 1985 Bermuda Bowl, São Paulo, Brazil. You're looking at

♠ K J 8 7 5 3   ♡ 9 8 3   ◇ J 9   ♣ J 3

with both sides vulnerable. Playing four-card majors, partner deals and surprises you with one spade. After Wolff makes a takeout double it's your turn. How many spades would you bid?

One year later... You're in the seat of the ubiquitous Pakistani star, Zia Mahmood. You've reached the finals of the 1986 Rosenblum Teams in Miami; you deal and hold

♠ K 9 7 4   ♡ 8 2   ◇ 8 6 5 2   ♣ 4 3 2

With both sides vulnerable, you pass to the 'bobbing and rocking' Kit Woolsey, of the United States, who opens with one diamond. Your partner overcalls one spade, and cerebral Ed Manfield on your right makes a careful negative double. It's up to you. Can you risk bidding with only three high-card points?

Most of the new teaching methods use the catchy theme of 'What strain and how high?' Pretty good questions. We don't rely on the LAW to tell us what strain (clubs, diamonds, etc.). As to 'How high?' — that's what the Law of Total Tricks was born for. In any competitive auction, if we know (or can estimate) the number of trumps, we'll have the answer to 'How high?'

We look now at the most important adjunct of the LAW:

> You should always bid to the level equal to the combined number of trumps held by your side.

If your side has eight trumps, you can contract for eight tricks and safely bid to the two-level. With nine trumps your side is safe at the three-level, and with ten trumps you can safely contract for ten tricks and bid to the four-level.

On the Hamman-Wolff deal, you can expect four spades from partner. Adding those to your six tells you to bid to the four-level. In his write-up of the São Paulo World Championships, Eric Kokish alluded to the LAW in his comments on the decision made by Austrian champion, Heinrich Berger. Berger jumped to three spades and then sold out to four hearts! Here are excerpts from Kokish's report: '...Berger had a lot of losers but, just the same, his three spades feels a trifle naive. The Law of Total Tricks would tend to confirm this... Wolff, who held

♠ Q ♡ A K Q 10 6 4 ◇ A 7 ♣ Q 10 5 2

was lucky because the auction hadn't turned out badly for him. What would he have done over 4♠-P-P to him?...'

Berger was -620 when he could have been -200 or -500 in four spades doubled, or even +100 against five hearts.

While it's safe to bid to the four-level with ten trumps, you won't always make what you bid; *but, even if you go down, you'll be sacrificing profitably against whatever the opponents can make.* This concept is so vital that it's worth making an effort to understand why it works.

Let's assume that our side has ten clubs. How many trumps will the opponents have? They have only three cards in clubs, leaving 23 of their 26 cards in the other suits. They must have an eight-card fit somewhere — the most balanced split possible in the remaining suits is 7+8+8=23. If we have ten clubs, and they have at least eight of something, there are at least 18 trumps, and 18 tricks. If we bid to the four-level with our ten clubs, and go down one, we have only nine tricks. Since the total is at least 18, the opponents must have at least nine tricks in their 'known' 8+ card fit. We are content to play in four clubs down one when the opponents can make three of their suit. Our ten clubs ensure us that, even if we can't make four clubs, we won't get a bad result, since they could have made their contract if left alone at the three-level. So, if we have ten trumps, we are safe to bid to the four-level.

Using the same logic, if we have nine trumps we can safely bid to the three-level. (This should tell you what to do with Zia's hand but we'll get back to that later.) Reasoning as we did above, we can see that, if we have nine trumps, they have only four cards in our suit, leaving 22 cards in the other suits. This again guarantees at least an eight-card fit for them (at least 8+7+7=22). Our nine trumps mean that the total is at least 17 trumps. Again, if we go down, we can expect that it was a good save against their contract. When we have nine trumps, there are going to be enough Total Tricks on the deal to protect us if we get to the three-level.

Of course, vulnerability and high-cards do have some relevance. You don't always want to get to the four-level vulnerable with no high cards, just because your side has ten trumps. Interestingly though, if a player blindly bid to the level of the number of trumps held by his side on every deal (totally ignoring vulnerability), he wouldn't do too badly. If your partner opens one spade (playing five-card majors), and you raise to four with

♠ 7 5 4 3 2 ♡ 5 3 ◇ K 6 5 ♣ 7 5 2

you might be considered too aggressive — but you will very often be making the winning bid. Give partner a typical hand like

♠ A K 9 8 6 ♡ A 6 2 ◇ Q 4 2 ♣ 10 3

and look what we have:

```
                    ♠ 7 5 4 3 2
                    ♡ 5 3
                    ◇ K 6 5
                    ♣ 7 5 2
  ♠ Q                   N          ♠ J 10
  ♡ Q J 9 8       W         E      ♡ K 10 7 4
  ◇ A J 8 3                        ◇ 10 9 7
  ♣ Q J 8 5             S          ♣ A K 9 4
                    ♠ A K 9 8 6
                    ♡ A 6 2
                    ◇ Q 4 2
                    ♣ 10 3
```

Yes, you'll go down in four spades, but they have a game in hearts! No surprise, is it? Look at what the LAW says: your side has ten spades and they have eight hearts, for a total of 18 trumps. You can take eight tricks in spades, so they should, and do, have ten tricks in hearts — for a total of 18 tricks.

Similarly, if partner opens one spade and you have

♠ Q J 4 2 ♡ 6 5 ◇ J 10 4 3 ♣ 8 6 3

the LAW says that you're safe in competing to three spades (nine trumps — nine tricks). We'd prefer not to be vulnerable, but let's give partner a very similar holding:

♠ A K 7 6 5   ♡ A 7 2   ◇ Q 6 2   ♣ 10 4

and see what we have:

♠ Q J 4 2	♠ A K 7 6 5
♡ 6 5	♡ A 7 2
◇ J 10 4 3	◇ Q 6 2
♣ 8 6 3	♣ 10 4

We won't make three spades, but think what the opponents can do with their eight-card fits. They will surely make nine or ten tricks in hearts (or clubs) depending on how suits split. We stand to gain a lot by bidding to the three-level with our nine trumps. Even if we can't make our contract, we can expect that there are enough Total Trumps and Tricks that the opponents would have made their contract.

To help us with our 'How high?' decision, we want to gear our bidding methods towards conveying the number of trumps we hold. No doubt, your own system already does a little of that. When you open one-of-a-major, you're telling your partner that you have at least five (unless you play four-card majors). When you open at the three-level, vulnerable against not, you're probably telling your partner that you have a seven-card suit. In this chapter, we'll take a look at some other ways to tell partner about our trump length. These are not esoteric ideas that occur once a year. Quite the contrary — they come up every session. Using these methods will make it easier for you and your partner to follow the LAW, and simple to answer the 'How high?' question — just get to the proper Law of Total Tricks level.

Here are some of the ways we get to the proper level:

1) Bergen raises
2) Preemptive raises in competition
3) Responding to Jacoby transfers
4) Preempting
5) D.O.N.T.
6) Support doubles
7) Unusual one notrump
8) Two-way Drury

1) BERGEN RAISES

Bergen raises gained a lot of popularity in the 1980's, but most of the players using them don't have any idea that they were invented because of the Law of Total Tricks ! They are designed specifically to get your side to the level of the number of trumps you hold, and are meant to be used with a five-card major system as follows:

PARTNER BIDS 1M AND THE OPPONENTS PASS:

2M	3-card support (7-10 points)	*Constructive*
2NT	4-card support (13+ points)	*Game-force*
3♣	4-card support (7-10 points)	*Constructive*
3◇	4-card support (10-12 points)	*Limit*
3M	4-card support (0-6 points)	*Preemptive*
4M	5-card support (0-7 points)	*Preemptive*

The other responses, and a more detailed explanation, can be found in other books such as *Better Bidding with Bergen*. Let's discuss the bids above, and how they pertain to the LAW.

Notice that with eight trumps we get only to the two-level (the two-level raise denies four-card support). With nine trumps, we bid immediately to the three-level irrespective of the strength or weakness of the hand. With ten trumps and a weak hand, we immediately get to the four-level. Not only do we want to get to the proper LAW level, but we want to get there as quickly as possible. Why should we leave room for the opponents to find out what they have, when we already know where we want to be?

With the weaker hands we take up the most space by raising our suit. We'd raise one spade to three with as little as

♠ J 10 4 2 ♡ 3 2 ◇ J 10 3 2 ♣ 5 4 3

— the LAW is the LAW. No matter how appalling you might think it is to bid three spades with this 'dog,' it's decidedly a long-run winning action. We make life miserable for the opponents, who have to come in at the four-level if they want to bid; and we do so safely — we have LAW protection!

In the same vein, we'd raise one spade to four with as little as

♠ J 10 5 4 3 ♡ 6 5 ♢ J 10 3 2 ♣ 4 3

— again believing in the LAW, and knowing that no matter how many we go down, they'd have had a compensatory score available if they had bid to their own contract. Yes, you could get a bad score jumping to four spades with such a weak hand — every now and then both sides will have only nine tricks. But it's far more likely that it's going to be their hand for game, or that you'll get lucky and make your contract on the wrong lead, or that they'll misjudge and do the wrong thing on the five-level, etc., etc. How do you like it when you hear 1♠–pass–4♠, holding

♠ 6 ♡ A K J 7 4 2 ♢ K 4 ♣ K Q 6 2?

The key concept to master is the meaning of 'LAW Protection.' You must keep in mind that when you bid to the level of the number of trumps held by your side:

> No matter how many tricks you go down, the LAW equation will see to it that there are enough Total Trumps on the deal to ensure that your opponents have a makable contract that is worth more than the penalty they'll collect defeating you.

2) PREEMPTIVE RAISES IN COMPETITION

When we have four-card support for partner's one-level over-call (usually a five-card suit), we immediately think in terms of getting to the three-level. We therefore use a jump-raise to show four trumps, weak. Its point range is approximately 0-7, depending upon vulnerability. We try not to have zero when we're vulnerable — but we keep in mind that they're not likely to be able to double and defend, since they won't have enough trumps. Even if they do, the LAW should protect us. Here's a typical layout, illustrating the deadly effect of the weak jump-raise:

Neither Vul.
Dealer West

```
                      ♠ Q 9 8
                      ♡ A K Q 5 4
                      ◇ 7 6 5
                      ♣ Q J
    ♠ A 5 4                              ♠ K 3 2
    ♡ 7 6            ┌─────────┐         ♡ 3 2
    ◇ A K 8 4        │    N    │         ◇ J 10 9 3
    ♣ A K 4 3        │  W   E  │         ♣ 9 7 6 5
                     │    S    │
                     └─────────┘
                      ♠ J 10 7 6
                      ♡ J 10 9 8
                      ◇ Q 2
                      ♣ 10 8 2
```

West	North	East	South
1◇	1♡	pass	3♡
dbl	pass	??	

West has no choice over three hearts except to double to show a good hand. We can see that if East guesses to pass the double, they'll beat us two for a good result. But do you know any player who would pass with that East hand? Could he risk passing when partner could easily have something like

♠ Q J 4 ♡ 4 ◇ A K 8 6 5 2 ♣ A K 4?

He'll probably bid four diamonds, and we'll end up with a plus score because of the preemptive jump.

If South had not jumped to three hearts, his side would surely have earned a minus score. If he'd 'gone slowly' with two hearts, the job would simply not have gotten done. West would double, East would bid three diamonds and, if North-South competed to three hearts, East-West would not be pushed to four diamonds.

By the way, there were only 17 trumps — if East had known that (and the LAW), he wouldn't have bid at the four-level. If he could take ten tricks, we'd only be taking seven. Notice, also, that there are actually only 16 tricks due to the minor honor adjustment in clubs. (More on this in Chapter Nine.)

The preemptive jump not only takes away the opposition's bidding room, it gives a proper description of your hand to partner. Suppose you're in fourth seat holding

♠ Q 6 5 4 ♡ 4 ◇ Q 6 4 2 ♣ 6 4 3 2

and hear **1◇–1♠–2♡**. Regardless of vulnerability, we would jump to three spades, preemptive. If you bid only two spades, how will you feel if they bid four hearts and partner doubles? Uncomfortable...? You should. You've created a problem for yourself, since you failed to describe your hand properly the first time. If you bid three spades, you get the whole hand 'off your chest,' and can abide by any decision partner makes for the rest of the auction.

Showing the fourth trump can reap benefits you might never have thought about. When Zia held

♠ K 9 7 4   ♡ 8 2   ◇ 8 6 5 2   ♣ 4 3 2

in Miami, he heard **1◇–1♠–dbl**. Vulnerable, he had no qualms about jumping to three spades. His counterpart in the other room (World Champion Bobby Lipsitz of the USA) faced the same auction and bid only two spades. The full deal:

Both Vul.
Dealer South

	♠ A J 10 6 3	
	♡ K 9 3	
	◇ —	
	♣ A Q J 10 9	

♠ Q	N	♠ 8 5 2
♡ Q J 10 5	W E	♡ A 7 6 4
◇ K Q 10 9 7 4	S	◇ A J 3
♣ K 6		♣ 8 7 5

	♠ K 9 7 4	
	♡ 8 2	
	◇ 8 6 5 2	
	♣ 4 3 2	

West	**North**	**East**	**South**
Woolsey	Fazli	Manfield	Zia
			pass
1◇	1♠	dbl	3♠
pass	4♠	all pass	

Fazli, expecting the four trumps, had an easy four-spade bid, and made five for +650. In the other room after the two-spade raise, the partnership ended in three spades making six! Notice, also, the preemptive effect of three spades — East-West were less able to investigate their profitable five-level sacrifice. The South hand looks pathetically weak for a vulnerable jump, but the

LAW dictates that it's safe to get to the three-level with nine trumps. Period. *End*!

What happens if we have four-card support, but more than preemptive strength? With a limit raise we can cuebid, but frequently a hand is not good enough for a limit raise but still too good to preempt. We call this a 'Mixed Raise.' For example, after **1♣–1♡–pass**, we're holding:

♠ K 5 3　♡ K J 10 3　◇ J 5 4 2　♣ 6 2

To show this Mixed Raise, *we jump cuebid in their suit* — three clubs. This is a good use for the normally unutilized jump cuebid. It gets us to the proper LAW level while taking up their bidding room and, at the same time, tells partner what we have.

Preemptive raises and Mixed Raises are still on even when the opponents' responder acts over the overcall. For example, after **1♣–1♡–1♠**, our raise to three hearts is still weak, and a jump to three clubs would still be a Mixed Raise.

While preemptive raises are an effective weapon, the original overcaller must be careful to follow the LAW himself. For example, consider the following hand, which most experts would misjudge.

In fourth seat, favorable at IMPs, you're holding:

♠ A J 5 3　♡ 5 3　◇ A K 6 3 2　♣ K 5

After two passes your RHO opens one club. You have several choices but elect to bid one diamond. After a negative double your partner makes a preemptive jump-raise to three diamonds, and the opener bids three hearts. It's up to you.

LHO	Partner	RHO	You
pass	pass	1♣	1◇
dbl	3◇	3♡	??

Most 'experts' would bid three spades 'on the way' to four diamonds. Why is this a mistake? The points are probably evenly split (about 20 for each side) so, if you pass, the auction is likely to end right here. You expect 17 trumps (eight for them and nine for you), so what good can come of bidding? If you get to four diamonds and make it (ten tricks), you were collecting +200 (seven tricks). If you take only nine tricks in four diamonds, you've turned +100 into -50. Granted, you have a good hand for a one-diamond overcall and you had hoped for better things, but there are not enough trumps to compete any further.

The full deal:

E-W Vul.
Dealer West

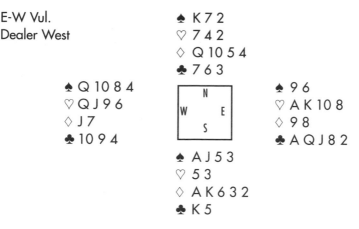

```
                    ♠ K 7 2
                    ♡ 7 4 2
                    ◇ Q 10 5 4
                    ♣ 7 6 3
    ♠ Q 10 8 4           N              ♠ 9 6
    ♡ Q J 9 6      W          E         ♡ A K 10 8
    ◇ J 7               S              ◇ 9 8
    ♣ 10 9 4                            ♣ A Q J 8 2
                    ♠ A J 5 3
                    ♡ 5 3
                    ◇ A K 6 3 2
                    ♣ K 5
```

3) RESPONDING TO JACOBY TRANSFERS

Another way we get to our proper LAW level is with our
responses to Jacoby transfers. We simply 'accept' the transfer if
we have only two or three cards in partner's major. However,
with four-card support we know that we have nine trumps, so
we 'super-accept' – we bid immediately to the three-level (what
else?). Granted, responder could be so weak that we'll go down
in three, but then we weren't buying the contract anyway. In
any decent bridge game, we're simply not going to be allowed
to 'steal' the contract on the two-level with nine trumps. So, we
don't mind getting 'pushed' to the three-level on our own, and
we don't want to give them time to get in a lead-directing bid,
or to find a good fit at the two-level in which they might be able
to compete successfully over three-of-our-major.

In general, we jump to three of responder's major with four
trumps and a minimum notrump. With extras (and four
trumps), we want to give partner some information, in case he
has a good hand, so we bid our doubleton; if we don't have a
doubleton (i.e. we're 4-3-3-3), then we bid two notrump. For
details on this treatment, see *Better Bidding with Bergen*.

Here's an example of the inhibiting effect 'super-accepting'
the transfer might have on the opposition:

Both Vul.
Dealer South

```
                    ♠ 5 2
                    ♡ Q J 10 8 6
                    ◇ K 6 4 2
                    ♣ 4 2
  ♠ A 8 7 3        ┌──────────┐        ♠ K J 10 6 4
  ♡ A 9 5          │    N     │        ♡ 4
  ◇ 8 5 3          │ W     E  │        ◇ J 10 7
  ♣ K J 8          │    S     │        ♣ Q 10 7 3
                   └──────────┘
                    ♠ Q 9
                    ♡ K 7 3 2
                    ◇ A Q 9
                    ♣ A 9 6 5
```

In a good pairs event, at most tables the auction would start

West	North	East	South
			1NT
pass	2◇	pass	2♡
pass	pass	??	

Any experienced East would balance with two spades. Now, even if we bid on to three hearts, West can bid three spades and score +140. Even if we're allowed to buy it in three hearts, we'll surely be held to +140 — the defense will have no trouble collecting their spade tricks when they come in with the ace of hearts.

With super-acceptances, the auction would be over in a hurry:

West	North	East	South
			1NT
pass	2◇	pass	3♡
all pass			

We'd score +140, or +170, instead of the -140 recorded by many of the other North-South pairs.

There's one other aspect of Jacoby Transfers we can turn to our advantage. When they double our transfer, we pass to show only two cards in responder's major — accepting shows three-card support. With four, we ignore the double and bid as above. Notice that our emphasis is, as always, on the number of trumps. *Telling partner about the trump fit is the most useful piece of information we can convey.*

Look how easy it is for North, holding

♠ J 9 3 ♡ K Q 9 5 3 ◇ 4 ♣ 10 6 4 3

after

West	North	East	South
			1NT
pass	2◇	dbl	pass[1]
3◇	??		

1. Only two hearts.

Knowing that his side has only a seven-card heart fit, he's not even tempted to bid three hearts.

4) PREEMPTING

The LAW can easily be applied to preempting. If you have a long suit, partner's expected length is one-third of the remaining cards in that suit. Everyone thinks it's okay to preempt on the three-level with a seven-card suit, and the LAW concurs — our side rates to have nine trumps (our seven plus partner's expected doubleton). Most players are also comfortable with a weak two-bid on a six-card suit — again validated by the LAW, since six, plus partner's expected 2⅓ (seven remaining cards divided among three players), adds up to more than eight trumps for our side. Only the modern generation thinks it's okay to open a weak two-bid with a five-card suit, but the LAW suggests that they're right! Partner's expectancy is 2⅔ (eight divided by three) — and approximately eight trumps for the partnership equals 'two-level safety.'

When we preempt we're gambling that, if the opponents choose to defend, they'll score less than if they'd had a free run to their own correct contract. As we can see, the LAW supports us. But, even granting that the initial bid may be a bit of a stab-in-the-dark, once we're in with a fit, responder will raise the pre-empt to the proper LAW level. The world often does this already. For example, they raise a weak two-bid to the three-level (preemptively) with three-card support. What they're doing is commendable. They're getting to the three-level with nine trumps — and the LAW is on their side.

Similarly, the LAW will be with you if you raise a seven-card three-spade opening to game with three-card support --regardless of your strength. You'll have ten trumps, so even if you go down the opponents would normally be able to make something their way. And think how tough it is with a good hand to have to enter the auction after **3♠–pass–4♠**!

An entire book could be written on the merits of aggressive preempting. While the world waits for six and seven-card suits, we get dealt five- and six-card suits much more often — so we preempt with those. But the point of this book is getting to the level dictated by the LAW. We want to be able to raise (or not raise) to the appropriate level, so as to safely put maximum pressure on the opponents. The key is to know how many trumps your partner has when he preempts. Then get to your proper LAW level — and get there quickly.

Let's say nobody is vulnerable and holding

♠ K 4 2   ♡ Q J 3   ◇ 5 4   ♣ K 5 4 3 2

you hear: **1◇–2♡–dbl** (RHO's double is negative). If partner's weak jump-overcall promises six hearts, then you have an easy three-heart bid. You don't expect to make it, but you don't care — you have nine trumps. The LAW is on your side.

Here's another hand. At favorable vulnerability you hold

♠ A 5   ♡ K 7 5 4 3   ◇ 6 5 4 3   ♣ 6 3

and hear this bidding: **1♣–2♡–dbl**. You should bid straight to the eleven-trick level — five hearts! That might be your instinctive bid anyway, but let's look at it LAW-wise. We have eleven trumps and they have at least eight somewhere (maybe nine). Let's pessimistically assume 19 trumps. If they double five hearts and beat us three tricks (eight for us), they'll have a certain game (11 tricks). If they beat us more, then they'll have a slam.

Some good players have a theory that bidding five hearts tells the opposition how well their hands fit, and therefore they pass and don't give information away. That might work, but it's much more effective to take away three levels of their space (including the Blackwood level) than it is to hope that both opponents will suddenly be struck deaf, dumb and blind!

Most players know to raise their partner's preempts even with a weak hand. Take, for example, the following deal from the 1984 Olympiad in Seattle:

N-S Vul.
Dealer East

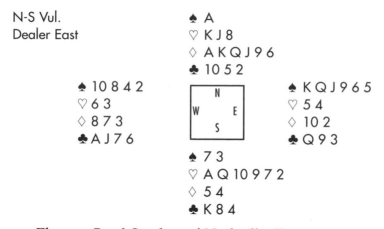

```
                        ♠ A
                        ♡ K J 8
                        ◇ A K Q J 9 6
                        ♣ 10 5 2
  ♠ 10 8 4 2          ┌─────────┐          ♠ K Q J 9 6 5
  ♡ 6 3               │    N    │          ♡ 5 4
  ◇ 8 7 3             │ W     E │          ◇ 10 2
  ♣ A J 7 6           │    S    │          ♣ Q 9 3
                      └─────────┘
                        ♠ 7 3
                        ♡ A Q 10 9 7 2
                        ◇ 5 4
                        ♣ K 8 4
```

    Elegant Carol Sanders of Nashville, Tennessee, opened the East hand with a weak two spades. After South passed, her long-time partner, Betty Ann Kennedy (who also hails from the Deep South), raised to four spades. This is the kind of bid that most good players would make instinctively, without realizing that the LAW is behind them. They just sensibly bid to the four-level with ten trumps.

    On the actual deal, the North player (amazingly!) passed four spades, and the final result was three down, undoubled, -150 — an embarrassment to North-South who have a twelve-top-tricks slam! Of course, you can't expect this kind of success just for obeying the LAW, but you will surely make life difficult for your opponents if you always take up their bidding space on this kind of a deal.

    In researching bridge deals from the 1970s and 1980s for this book, I found two noteworthy trends concerning preempting. The first was the increasing frequency — the later the year, the more preempts there were. The other noticeable trend was that aggressive preempting proved to be a winning action. Roughly 60-70% of the time, an aggressive preempt was more successful than the conservative action chosen at the other table(s). There are countless examples to choose from, but only one deal will be presented here. It isn't special in any way, just a typical, every-day representation of the trend:

Neither Vul.
Dealer West

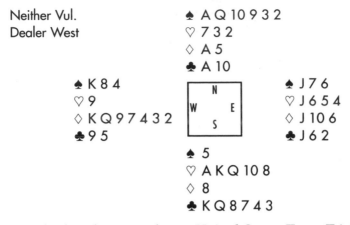

```
                  ♠ A Q 10 9 3 2
                  ♡ 7 3 2
                  ◇ A 5
                  ♣ A 10
♠ K 8 4                              ♠ J 7 6
♡ 9                                  ♡ J 6 5 4
◇ K Q 9 7 4 3 2                      ◇ J 10 6
♣ 9 5                                ♣ J 6 2
                  ♠ 5
                  ♡ A K Q 10 8
                  ◇ 8
                  ♣ K Q 8 7 4 3
```

The hand occurred in a United States Team Trials. At one table, West dealt and passed. The traditional wisdom was that his hand was 'flawed' — a weakish suit, and Kxx in a side major, meant you weren't supposed to preempt. Nowadays, most players realize that waiting for

♠ 3 2   ♡ 2   ◇ K Q J 10 9 6 3   ♣ 4 3 2

(a 'classic' preempt) is a losing proposition.

After West's disciplined pass, his expert opponents bid very well indeed, and scored +1520 in seven notrump. At the other table, the East-West pair was more in step with the modern times. West opened three diamonds and North overcalled with three spades. East raised to four diamonds, and South guessed wrong to bid only four hearts, which ended the auction — a 15 IMP swing. East-West were never in danger — they would still have gained 12 IMPs if they had been doubled at the four-level (with their ten trumps).

Constructive bidding in the new century is exceptionally sophisticated — you can't afford to give the opposition a free run repeatedly. Left to themselves, they will usually reach their correct contract. It should be your goal to interrupt their auction whenever you can safely do so, and preempting is the most effective way to disturb their communications. But, it is imperative not to abuse the Law of Total Tricks. Be aggressive, but keep the ultimate goal in mind: *The partnership should strive to preempt to exactly the level of their combined number of trumps.*

5) D.O.N.T.

Interfering after the opponents have opened one notrump is an indispensable area of good competitive bidding. In the old days, you needed quite a good hand to bid over an opponent's strong notrump. As time went by, a lot of conventions sprang up — Landy, Astro, Brozel, Cappelletti, etc. This proliferation of conventions emerged from the frustration of one bad result after another from passing out one notrump. You frequently lead the wrong suit and/or have a difficult time with the defense. Later, you discover that your side could have made a two-level contract if you had competed. As well, passing in the direct seat allows the opponents an accurate auction — most pairs have good constructive methods after their own one-notrump opening.

Interfering is clear. The question is how best to do it. The idea should be to safely enter the auction and find a playable spot, while giving your side the best chance to locate an 8+ card fit. Getting to a makable game should be of little concern. Bidding over their notrump has little to do with high-card points — it should be based primarily on shape. Even if you have zero(!) high-card points, the LAW will protect you if you can find an eight-card fit on the two-level.

For these reasons, we think D.O.N.T. is the best way to interfere. D.O.N.T. is Marty Bergen's acronym for 'Disturbing Opponents' No Trump.' And that is exactly our goal — to disturb! Yes, we want to find our right contract but, at all costs we want to prevent them from playing in one notrump, or from having a good Stayman or Jacoby sequence.

Disturbing Opponents NoTrump (direct and balancing seat):

dbl   Any one-suiter — partner must pull to two clubs. We will pass with clubs, otherwise bid our suit.

2♣   Clubs and a higher suit

2◊   Diamonds and a major

2♡   Both majors

2♠   Spades (weaker than double followed by two spades)

Notice that we show all one and two-suiters without getting to the three-level. Any possible eight-card fit can be found, and played, at the two-level — a delight as far as the LAW is concerned.

Most methods put the accent on getting to a major, but that should not be your goal. Getting to a major matters when looking for game, or trying for the best possible plus on a partscore deal at matchpoints. You have a different goal when intervening against one notrump: *disturb the opponents as often as is feasible, and as safely as possible.* D.O.N.T. will often allow you to find a safe haven in two clubs or two diamonds. Almost all other conventions are inferior in this regard. They find minor-suit fits, but force you to play at the three-level. Unless you're lucky enough to have a nine-card fit, the LAW says you don't want to be at that level!

Some methods allow you to make a penalty double of one notrump. Are we bothered by the fact that D.O.N.T. doesn't allow for this? Not at all! Penalty doubles of one notrump are unappealing and ineffective. Choosing an opening lead and defending against one notrump doubled is one of the most difficult challenges in bridge. Furthermore, it's rare to be dealt a strong hand when an opponent also has a strong hand. And even if you can double and defeat one notrump, the opponents will often have a place to run and the mechanism to get there. Not only can they run out but, after your penalty double, they'll have a way to play in two clubs or two diamonds — unreachable contracts if one notrump is not doubled! On top of everything else, there is no need to double with a big balanced hand — we can pass and let partner balance if he has shape.

Here is a typical deal which illustrates how futile penalty doubles of one notrump tend to be:

Neither Vul.
Dealer East

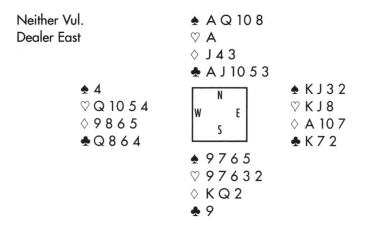

♠ A Q 10 8
♡ A
♢ J 4 3
♣ A J 10 5 3

♠ 4
♡ Q 10 5 4
♢ 9 8 6 5
♣ Q 8 6 4

♠ K J 3 2
♡ K J 8
♢ A 10 7
♣ K 7 2

♠ 9 7 6 5
♡ 9 7 6 3 2
♢ K Q 2
♣ 9

When this hand was played in the Round Robin of the 1985 Bermuda Bowl in São Paulo, nearly all tables started 1NT (by East) followed by two passes. Some Norths, who made a penalty double, ended up -180 after a heart lead and spade switch. If North had bid D.O.N.T. (two clubs), South would have bid two diamonds, telling North to show his other suit. North would have bid two spades and done quite well there.

Obviously, North had plenty of points and found it easy to balance, but we would balance even if both major suit aces were deuces! Balancing after 1NT and two passes is a very much misunderstood position by the average player. Most good players are alert to the fact that bids in passout seat can be made on very weak hands. When the opponents pass their one-notrump opening, they're telling you that they have at most around 23 high-card points. If they had more, the responder would have taken some action. So, our side is known to have at least 17, or almost half the deck. How those 17 are divided between the balancer and his partner is irrelevant; what matters is that the player with shape gets his side into the bidding. Suppose direct seat has a 4-3-3-3 twelve-count, and the balancer has a 5-5-2-1 five-count. The bidding should go **1NT–pass–pass**, and now balancer should show his two-suiter. As long as neither partner gets carried away trying for game, everything will be all right.

Bidding in direct seat with very few points is not advisable because the responder to one notrump is unlimited. But **1NT–pass–pass** is a glowing invitation for the player in balancing seat to bid with any kind of decent distribution. The partnership will have enough high-card points to be competing.

Over the years, balancing against one notrump has proven to be extremely successful. On the other hand, passing out one notrump and watching partner lead the suit in which we have a small doubleton has not been rewarding — or pleasant.

On the following deal from the 1980 World Team Olympiad in Valkenburg, the American East-West pair were not in sync in a match against France:

Neither Vul.   ♠ K J 5
Dealer North   ♡ A 6 3
                 ◊ Q 6 2
                 ♣ A Q 7 2

```
       ♠ K J 5
       ♡ A 6 3
       ◊ Q 6 2
       ♣ A Q 7 2
♠ Q 8 6 3              ♠ 10 9 7 2
♡ 10 8 7 5 2    N      ♡ K Q
◊ 7           W   E    ◊ A K J 10 5 3
♣ K J 4          S     ♣ 10
       ♠ A 4
       ♡ J 9 4
       ◊ 9 8 4
       ♣ 9 8 6 5 3
```

West	North	East	South
Soloway	*Mari*	*I. Rubin*	*Chemla*
	1NT	pass	pass
2♣	pass	4♠	all pass

Soloway-Rubin were using Landy — two clubs showed majors. They found their eight-card fit all right, but they weren't on the same wavelength. This wasn't a question of methods, but of philosophy: Soloway should have been allowed to balance without getting himself hung by 'The Beast.' North-South would probably make one notrump (on a high diamond lead) and East-West could make two spades. Playing D.O.N.T., we might have bid in direct seat, but even if we passed, we wouldn't bury partner for balancing by trying to get to a game.

For readers who want to play D.O.N.T. (all of you, I hope) and insist on trying to get to game (don't say I didn't warn you), the response of two notrump to a D.O.N.T. overcall is a game-try. (Overcaller uses the next four steps to show his other suit and whether he is minimum or maximum at the same time.) But please go out of your way to allow the overcaller leeway; be judicious in your use of the two-notrump ask. Don't risk getting to the three-level and undoing the good work of the D.O.N.T. overcall — you're often already ahead of the 'field.' Getting to game the one time in ten that it makes will gain one swing and lose nine!

Playing D.O.N.T. with this partnership philosophy is an awesome mechanism for dealing with the opponents' notrump opening. With the Law of Total Tricks as the underlying support, many good results can be chalked up. In Chapter Seven, 'Notrump and the LAW,' we'll see further evidence of why we *do* play D.O.N.T.

6) SUPPORT DOUBLES

This modern bidding method is tailor-made to fit with the Law of Total Tricks . Support doubles were created by Eric Rodwell who, at the age of 17 (before he'd won so much as a sectional tournament), needed to protect himself from his own youthful exuberance. After a nebulous Precision one-diamond opening, he was fond of responding one-of-a-major with a three-card suit, but less fond of playing in a three-three fit, when his innocent partner raised. He decided that a raise in competition had to show four trumps, so to distinguish three-card support from four, his partner would double with only three.

A Support Double occurs when you open the bidding, and partner responds with one-of-a-new-suit (whether or not second hand has bid). If RHO makes any bid, up to and including two of responder's suit, opener doubles to show three-card support, or raises to show four. For example, after

West	North	East	South
1◊	pass	1♡	2♣
??			

opener can double to show three hearts. His raise to two hearts shows four-card support.

A Support Redouble is essentially the same. The only difference is that RHO has made a takeout double, rather than an overcall. After

West	North	East	South
1♣	pass	1♠	dbl
??			

opener redoubles with three spades; bidding two spades shows four of them. The Support Double (or Redouble) sends no message about strength, but it has a hidden advantage — opener will get a chance to bid again when he has a strong hand, since his partner is 'forced' to bid. The Support Double gives up a penalty double, but that's a small price to pay. Responder will always know his side's combined trump length, enabling him to make quite accurate LAW decisions.

7) UNUSUAL ONE NOTRUMP

What's wrong with this deal from the 1985 Bermuda Bowl?

Neither Vul.
Dealer West

```
                      ♠ Q 5 4 2
                      ♡ A 8 7
                      ◇ A Q J 10 8
                      ♣ A
    ♠ 10 9 8                          ♠ J
    ♡ Q J 6 2          ┌─────────┐    ♡ K 5 4
    ◇ 9                │    N    │    ◇ 7 5 4 3
    ♣ K Q 7 6 3      W │       E │      ♣ J 10 9 5 2
                       │    S    │
                       └─────────┘
                      ♠ A K 7 6 3
                      ♡ 10 9 3
                      ◇ K 6 2
                      ♣ 8 4
```

West	North	East	South
Monsegur	*Frydrich*	*Mooney*	*Hochzeit*
pass	1◇	pass	1♠
pass	2♡	pass	2♠
pass	3♠	pass	4◇
pass	5NT	pass	6◇
pass	6♠	pass	7♠
all pass			

Yes, there are more tricks than trumps, but that will be explained in Chapter Nine. Something else is troubling about this deal. Let's look first at some competitive bidding theory...

Nearly everyone likes Unusual Two Notrump — it jams the opponents and gives your side a good chance to compete if you have a fit. We like the concept so much that we also use it on the one-level. After **1x–pass–1y**, we use both one notrump and two notrump to show the unbid suits. When we don't have enough shape to feel comfortable getting to the three-level, we bid one notrump. After **1◇–pass–1♡**, if we have

♠ Q J 10 9   ♡ x x   ◇ x x   ♣ K Q 10 9 x

we wouldn't dream of passing. We love to get in with one notrump. Often enough, partner will have some normal balanced hand and be able to compete to two spades or three clubs, when the opponents were about to stop in two hearts.

We don't mind giving up a natural one notrump when they've opened and responded — it's a risky action at best, and the strong notrump hand has a much lower frequency than a weakish two-suiter. Again, the LAW is the guiding principle behind our desire to get into the auction. It's safe to compete to the two-level by entering with one notrump, because the LAW will protect us when we have a fit. Bids that show two different suits give us a very good chance to find a fit — which we think is enough of a reason to be in the auction.

When we're lucky enough to find a good fit, partner jumps to the three- or four-level to preempt, confident in LAW protection. This kind of auction is especially gratifying because the 'field' isn't getting in, and the fit gets lost at other tables. Another benefit of Unusual One Notrump is that, if partner makes a takeout double when he had one notrump available as a light distributional takeout, he promises a fairly decent hand in high-cards.

Here's a hand where we'd bid one notrump at matchpoints with both sides vulnerable:

♠ 10 4   ♡ Q J 8 6 4   ◇ K Q 10 5 3   ♣ 2

LHO	Partner	RHO	You
1♣	pass	1♠	??

While two notrump would be an aggressive (but possibly successful) tactic, we'd prefer to enter more 'safely' with one notrump to show our light two-suiter. Some experts would consider this unsound — it might give the opponents a key to the distribution or a good chance for a penalty. But in my experience, a more likely scenario is:

Both Vul.
Dealer West

```
                    ♠ A J 9 5
                    ♡ 10 3
                    ◇ A J 6 2
                    ♣ J 6 3
  ♠ Q 2                              ♠ K 8 7 6 3
  ♡ K 7 2          N                 ♡ A 9 5
  ◇ 9 4       W         E            ◇ 8 7
  ♣ A Q 9 7 5 4          S           ♣ K 10 8
                    ♠ 10 4
                    ♡ Q J 8 6 4
                    ◇ K Q 10 5 3
                    ♣ 2
```

At many tables the auction might be:

West	North	East	South
1♣	pass	1♠	pass
2♣	pass	3♣	all pass

East-West would probably be +110 in clubs, while North-South could have made 110 in diamonds.

At our table South would bid one notrump and North would compete in diamonds, ensuring a good result for North-South. The North hand is fairly representative of what South could hope for — as opposed to the gloomy

♠ A J 9 5   ♡ 10 3   ◇ 6 2   ♣ K J 6 4 3

that the passing pessimists might expect!

Let's return to São Paulo and the deal that started this discussion. The Argentines watched quietly as their opponents bid, unobstructed, to seven spades. West held

♠ 10 9 8   ♡ Q J 6 2   ◇ 9   ♣ K Q 7 6 3

with nobody vulnerable, and heard **1◇–pass–1♠**. He passed, as would most players, where we would have bid one notrump. Our partner, holding

♠ J   ♡ K 5 4   ◇ 7 5 4 3   ♣ J 10 9 5 2

would have jumped preemptively to four clubs, making it unlikely that the Israelis would reach the grand slam. In fact, none of the North-South pairs who received interference were able to reach it. Unusual One Notrump would have saved the day for East-West. Entering the auction at a low-level with two suits is an excellent, and safe way to get your side into the Law of Total Tricks picture.

8) TWO-WAY DRURY

Drury is a popular convention in which a two-club bid is used after a third or fourth-seat one-of-a-major opening. It's designed to give the passed hand a way to show a limit raise without getting the partnership to the three-level. We especially don't want to be at the three-level with only eight trumps, so we use both two-club and two-diamond responses by a passed hand to show a limit raise with three- and four-card support respectively. Opener will know his side's combined trump length and be able to make accurate LAW decisions. Interested readers can find a full explanation of Two-way Drury in *Better Bidding with Bergen*.

All of the ideas in this chapter require partnership discussion and cooperation. The effort is worth it. The cumulative effect, over session after session of quickly bidding up to the level of your trump fit, is astounding!

You won't always notice as it's happening, but you'll find that, more and more, your opponents will be struggling to find the right spot, and will often end up in silly contracts. They'll be guessing wrong — bidding at the four-level when there are only 17 trumps, or competing in their seven-card fit instead of their eight-card fit, because they had no room to explore. They'll defend against your three-spade contract and beat you two tricks, but be cold for four hearts — and never have had a safe opportunity to get into the bidding. You'll be -50 on a lot of hands when the 'field' is -110, -130, or -140, because they didn't make life tough enough for their opponents. You'll keep winning 5 IMPs at a time because you've pushed them around on the partscore deals. And on, and on, and on...

Many bridge writers are highly critical of aggressive actions

— and sometimes those actions do look a bit silly when they lead to -500 against nothing. It's easy to point to 'errors' of *commission*. But, the players who just sit there and pass, and let their opponents bid easily to the right contract, don't come in for much criticism for their errors of *omission*. They just say, 'We did poorly because our opponents played well — they did everything right.' Or, 'There was no way to have a good session — every one played good bridge — my opponents always got to the right contract.' Another popular phrase is, 'We were dealt a bad game.' I think there's no such thing!

I don't want to allow my opponents to 'play well.' Would it be good tactics, in any competitive activity, to just sit there and not put up any defense? You have to get in there and make it tough for the enemy. You'll get burned every now and then, but more often than not, you'll push them into the wrong spot. Use the LAW to guide you — when your side has a fit, it's so easy. Just get to the proper LAW level and let the chips fall where they may — usually into your pile!

CHAPTER REVIEW

- The Law of Total Tricks says that you can safely bid to the level equal to the number trumps held by your side.

- The premise we rely on for bidding to our LAW level is called 'LAW Protection.' By this we mean that we are protected because, even if we go down in our contract, we expect that there are enough trumps on the deal that the opponents could have made a contract of their own.

- Some of the methods that we use to bid to our LAW level are:

  1) Bergen raises: Designed to tell partner our strength and, more importantly, our number of trumps.

  2) Preemptive raises: Designed to get us to the proper LAW level in competition.

  3) Jacoby Transfer responses: Getting to the three-level immediately with 9+ trumps.

  4) Preempting: With the accent on the number of trumps and bidding to the corresponding level.

  5) D.O.N.T. : The best way to compete over one notrump is to be able to show all one- and two-suiters at a safe level.

  6) Support doubles: To tell partner whether we have three- or four-card support.

  7) Unusual 1NT: To get into the auction and try to find a fit at a safe level.

  8) Two-way Drury: To show three- or four-card support.

1) If our side has a nine-card fit, why are we safe to bid to the three-level? What fit will the opponents have?

2) What is the theory behind Bergen raises?

3) What would you do with each of the following? (assume you're playing IMPs with both sides vulnerable):

LHO	Partner	RHO	You
a)	3♡	pass	??

♠ 8 5　♡ 9 7 3　♢ A Q 3　♣ K 8 7 5 2

LHO	Partner	RHO	You
b)	2♠	dbl	??

♠ K 7 6　♡ K 4 2　♢ A 9 8　♣ 5 4 3 2

LHO	Partner	RHO	You
c) pass	1♠	dbl	??

♠ J 10 8 3　♡ 5 4　♢ 10 9 7 5 2　♣ 9 3

4) What would you bid with each of the following? Assume nobody is vulnerable and the bidding has gone:

LHO	Partner	RHO	You
1♢	1♡	pass	??

a) ♠ A 4 2　♡ K 5 4　♢ 6 4 3　♣ Q 7 5 2
b) ♠ 6 5 4　♡ K 7 6 2　♢ 4 3　♣ J 7 5 2
c) ♠ A 6 3　♡ K 7 5 3　♢ 4 3　♣ J 10 7 3
d) ♠ A 5 3　♡ Q 7 5 3　♢ 4 3　♣ A J 5 2
e) ♠ 3 2　♡ K 7 5 4 3　♢ 4　♣ 6 5 4 3 2

5) Your RHO opens one notrump (15-17) and you're playing matchpoints at favorable vulnerability. Playing D.O.N.T. what do you bid with each of the following hands?

a) ♠ 5 3　♡ A 5 3　♢ Q J 9 8　♣ K Q 10 4
b) ♠ A J 10 5 3　♡ Q J 9 3　♢ 5 4 3　♣ 2
c) ♠ A Q J 9 6 5　♡ 7 5 4　♢ 4 2　♣ 3 2
d) ♠ 4 2　♡ Q 10 9 5　♢ 6 4　♣ K Q 10 6 3
e) ♠ K 5 4　♡ Q J 9 3　♢ Q J 9 4　♣ Q 4

6) You're playing D.O.N.T. , and your LHO opens one notrump (15-17). It's IMPs with nobody vulnerable.

LHO	Partner	RHO	You
1NT	2♣	pass	??

What should you do with each of the following?

a) ♠ A 4 ♡ K 6 4 2 ◇ Q 7 4 3 ♣ K 4 2
b) ♠ 6 4 3 2 ♡ 7 5 4 3 ◇ 6 5 3 2 ♣ 2
c) ♠ Q J 6 5 3 ♡ Q J 6 4 3 ◇ — ♣ 5 3 2
d) ♠ 6 3 ♡ 4 3 ◇ 7 5 4 2 ♣ A 6 5 3 2

7) Again, you're playing D.O.N.T. and hear this auction:

LHO	Partner	RHO	You
		1NT	pass
pass	2♡	pass	??

What should you do with each of the following?

a) ♠ A 6 4 ♡ Q 5 4 ◇ 6 4 3 2 ♣ 5 4 3
b) ♠ A 7 5 4 ♡ Q 5 4 ◇ K 4 3 ♣ 5 4 3
c) ♠ 4 3 ♡ 5 2 ◇ A Q J 4 3 ♣ Q J 10 3

CHAPTER 4 ANSWERS

1) We are safe because of 'LAW Protection.' Our nine trumps guarantee that the opponents have at least eight trumps, and that if we have only eight tricks, they will have nine.

2) To get to the two-level with eight trumps and to the three-level with nine trumps (i.e. the LAW is behind Bergen raises).

3)   a) Four hearts. Partner's seven plus our three equals ten — four-level.

  b) Three spades. Partner's six plus our three equals nine — three-level.

  c) Three spades. Partner's five plus our four equals nine — three-level.

4)   a) Two hearts. With eight trumps bid to the two-level.

  b) Three hearts. With nine trumps get to the three-level.

    c) Three diamonds. Mixed Raise — nine trumps, so get to the three-level, but too good for a preemptive raise.

    d) Two diamonds — too good for a Mixed Raise. We will compete to the three-level if necessary.

    e) Four hearts. With ten trumps bid to the four-level.

5)   **a)** Two clubs — your suits are adequate to try to disturb the opponents. Some bridge 'experts' will not like your action! (Gives away too much..., too risky, etc. etc.). I enjoy playing against such 'experts'.

    b) Two hearts — show both majors. You're not promising a lot of high cards.

    c) Two spades — takes up room, and partner knows we don't have too much because we'd double and then bid two spades with more.

    d) Two clubs — delighted to be able to get in so cheaply.

    e) Pass — we must have some standards!

6)   **a)** Pass — we might have a game, but that's not enough of a reason to try for anything else. Be happy we interfered.

    b) Two diamonds — partner will pass with diamonds, or bid his major.

    c) Pass — don't go looking for trouble. Even if partner has a major, we might already be ahead of the field just by being in the bidding — and partner probably has diamonds!

    d) Three clubs — we have at least nine. We're not looking for game — just trying to make it hard for the opponents to compete. With a real invitation we'd inquire with two notrump.

7)   **a)** Pass — no reason to disturb two undoubled hearts.

    b) Two spades — yes, we have a nice hand, but we don't hang partner for balancing.

    c) ?? Why didn't we bid two clubs over 1NT?

OFF THE PROPER LEVEL

CHAPTER 5

In the previous chapter we discussed some ways to get to the-level suggested by the Law of Total Tricks. It's every bit as important to prevent the opponents from playing at their proper LAW level. We learned an important adjunct of the LAW which told us that we are safe to bid to the-level of the number of trumps that we have between us. To carry it one step further:

> Try not to let the opponents play at a level equal to their number of trumps.

If they have an eight-card fit, and are at the two-level, they are in good shape — the LAW tells them that. We want to try very hard to never sell out at the two-level, if we believe that they have eight trumps. If you think about it, if they have eight trumps, we too are very likely to have eight trumps somewhere. The only way we won't have an 8+ card fit is if our 26 cards are distributed exactly 5-7-7-7.

If we have eight trumps, and they have eight, and the points are relatively 'evenly' distributed, we can't afford to let them play at the two-level. Let's say they're playing five-card majors and bid as follows:

Opener	Responder
1♡	2♡
pass	

We know several things. One is that they have at least an eight-card fit. Also, the points are 'evenly' distributed. They're not stopping in two hearts with 25+ high card points — so we know that our side has at least reasonable strength. We also know that, as far as the LAW is concerned, they are in excellent shape on the two-level. There are usually going to be 16 total trumps, and we can reason as follows:

- If they're making exactly two, then we can also take eight tricks, if we play in our suit.

- If they're making an overtrick, then we can take seven tricks (down one in two spades, or down two on the three-level).

- If they're going down, then we can make at least nine tricks!

As you can see, it's imperative that we don't let them play in two hearts. The odds heavily favor us getting into the auction — even if we have to go to the three-level, we'll only get hurt badly if they can double and collect a penalty worth more than their partscore.

Matchpoint players instinctively 'balance' on this type of auction — but the advantages at IMPs are even greater! You can often push them to three of their suit, down one, or else both partscores may be making. Even when you go minus, you won't lose anything if they were making two hearts. And best of all, at IMPs they'll be very reluctant to double you into game, whereas at matchpoints you're much more susceptible to getting punished with a double.

Not letting the opponents play in eight-card fits at the two-level is so crucial that we have 'methods' for preventing it. In this chapter we will explore the following ways of getting the opponents out of their two-level fit:

1) OBAR BIDS
2) Scrambling 2NT
3) 'Super' Unusual 2NT
4) Good-bad 2NT
5) Aggressive minor-suit raises

1) OBAR BIDS

This acronym, invented by Marty Bergen, stands for 'Opponents Bid And Raise — Balance In Direct Seat.' What this means is that we consider the direct seat to be almost the same as the balancing seat. Balancing normally refers to this situation:

Partner	RHO	You	LHO
pass	1♡	pass	2♡
pass	pass	??	

They've stopped in two hearts, and we'd consider it a crime to pass — it's very safe to balance, since you know your side has some strength, and you know that the LAW will protect you.

But, even in direct seat we try to 'balance'. Direct seat refers to the player who bids immediately after the two-heart raise. We consider it safe to bid even in direct seat, because we have 'LAW Protection'. There will be enough Total Trumps and Tricks to warrant competing. You don't need a lot of points to **Balance In Direct Seat** — you just need shape. Let's consider the merits of balancing in direct seat with a five-card spade suit after 1♡ - **pass** - 2♡.

Certainly, if the strength is 'evenly' divided, we've already seen that it's okay to enter the auction. But, even if it's their hand, and they're about to bid a game, you'll still survive. In most cases, they'll just ignore you and bid their game anyway — nobody likes to dig in to defending a doubled partscore when they have a game to bid. Even if they do decide to double you, they'll have to beat you enough tricks to make up for their game bonus. If it goes 1♡ - **pass** - 2♡, and you bid two spades (and each side has eight trumps), look what happens if they double you when they have a game:

Vul.	Score for 4♡ taking 10 tricks	Score for 2♠ doubled taking only 6 tricks
Favorable	−620	**−300**
Neither	−420	**−300**
Both	−620	**−500**
Unfavorable	**−420**	−500

Only at unfavorable vulnerability do we get hurt — so we just try to be a little more cautious at those colors.

Notice that we assumed 16 trumps — not a bad assumption. Yes, we could be unlucky enough to have only seven, but then maybe they'll have nine. Even if there are only 15 trumps, it's not often that they can double — they will usually bid game if they think they can make it.

A huge advantage of **Balancing In Direct Seat** is that you can get in a lead-directing bid. After 1♡ - **pass** - 2♡, we'd gladly bid two spades in direct seat with as little as

♠ K Q J 9 3   ♡ 4 3   ◇ 4 3 2   ♣ 4 3 2

This might go against everything you were taught — but look at the reasons:

a) We're dying for a spade lead — how would you feel if you passed, and they raised to four hearts? You'd sit there hoping (praying) for a spade lead.

b) We know it's right to 'balance'. Any good player holding this hand in the real balancing seat would routinely bid two spades. Why should we pass it around to partner who might balance with three clubs holding

♠ 10 4 2   ♡ 7 6 5   ◇ A Q   ♣ K Q 10 6 5

We're the one who knows it's right to introduce spades.

c) Partner won't punish us. He knows we are playing OBAR BIDS. We're not trying to get to game when they open and raise. Yes, there are exceptions, but at least 90% of the time, when they open and raise, we don't have to worry about our side bidding and making a game. Besides, partner couldn't act over one heart — what's he going to do all of a sudden? Bid a game just because of our simple overcall? He shouldn't play us for high-cards and do something silly — like double them if they bid on. He knows that we are just 'balancing'.

d) What's the downside? Is it really likely that they will double and beat us more than the value of two hearts? How often do you think one of them will have four cards in our suit? It's very unlikely. Partner probably has a few cards in every suit (he couldn't bid a long suit over their opening bid) — and they have 8+ of their 26 cards in their suit. It's just plain against all the odds that they'll have a side four-card suit specifically in your long suit!

It's prudent to avoid bidding a suit in direct seat if you have a weak hand and a bad suit. You wouldn't want to bid two spades over **1♡ - pass - 2♡** with

♠ J 6 4 3 2   ♡ A 4 2   ◇ A 3   ♣ 6 4 2

Partner will not be happy with you when he leads the king of spades from Kx against three hearts! Furthermore, it's easier for the opponents to double when you have a bad suit.

Even if we can't overcall in direct seat, we still try hard to 'pre-balance' with a double if we have the right shape. Let's say we have:

♠ A 6 4 3 ♡ 6 ◇ K 9 8 4 ♣ Q J 6 2

and it goes 1♡ - **pass** - 2♡. If we pass it around to partner, how's he going to feel about balancing when he's looking at

♠ K 7 5 ♡ J 9 8 3 ◇ Q J 7 5 ♣ K 5

We have the hand with the proper shape to get into the bidding — so we 'balance' in the direct seat. What kind of result do you think you'd get for defending two hearts if this were the full deal:

```
                    ♠ 10 9 2
                    ♡ A 5 4
                    ◇ 3 2
                    ♣ A 10 9 8 7
    ♠ K 7 5                          ♠ A 6 4 3
    ♡ J 9 8 3         N              ♡ 6
    ◇ Q J 7 5      W     E           ◇ K 9 8 4
    ♣ K 5             S              ♣ Q J 6 2
                    ♠ Q J 8
                    ♡ K Q 10 7 2
                    ◇ A 10 6
                    ♣ 4 3
```

If East passes the raise to two hearts, he's not going to get a very good result. North-South can make two hearts, and East-West will do quite well either playing in three diamonds or pushing North-South to three hearts, down one. This is a very typical layout. Yes, on rare occasions, something bad happens to us when we 'balance' in direct seat. Sometimes we go for a number, or give away the location of key cards — but bridge is a game of percentages. We want to be 'right' on the *majority* of the hands. The preceding hand is representative of the majority. At all forms of scoring, we've shown a huge profit over the long haul by getting into this kind of auction. We don't get discouraged the one time in ten that we're wrong.

Balancing **I**n **D**irect **S**eat also applies to the following auctions, where logic dictates that both players are really in 'balancing seat':

Opener	Responder
1NT	2♣
2◇	3♣[1]

1. Sign-off.

Opener	Responder
pass	1♠
2♣[1]	2♠[2]

1. Drury.
2. Sign-off.

Opener	Responder
1NT	2NT[1]
3♣[2]	3◇[3]

1. Transfer to diamonds.
2. Maximum.
3. Sign-off.

Opener	Responder
1NT	2♡[1]

1. Natural, weak.

Opener	Responder
2♡	2♠[1]

1. Non-forcing.

Opener	Responder
1◇[1]	2♡[2]

1 Limited (playing a forcing club system).
2. Weak.

The following is the kind of run-of-the-mill deal where 5 to 6 IMPs are often at stake:

N-S Vul.
Dealer West

```
                    ♠ Q 7 6
                    ♡ A K 8 5 4
                    ◇ Q 9
                    ♣ K J 8
  ♠ J 10 9 4                        ♠ A 8 5 3 2
  ♡ 7 6 2         ┌──────────┐      ♡ Q J 10
  ◇ A J 5 3 2     │    N     │      ◇ K 6
  ♣ 4             │  W   E   │      ♣ A 7 2
                  │    S     │
                  └──────────┘
                    ♠ K
                    ♡ 9 3
                    ◇ 10 8 7 4
                    ♣ Q 10 9 6 5 3
```

When this deal was played in the 1984 World Championships in Seattle, North-South bid unopposed to three clubs and scored +110, on the following auction:

West	North	East	South
Romanski	Terraneo	Tuszynski	Fucik
pass	1NT	pass	2♣
pass	2♡	pass	3♣
all pass			

Obviously, the hand belongs to East-West in spades (they can make ten tricks, but just getting to three spades is sufficient), yet they went -110. What went wrong?

West counted high-card points instead of trumps. He was alerted that South's three clubs was a sign-off. He knew the opponents had a club fit of eight, nine, or even ten cards in length. He could also expect that his side had a fit somewhere — probably at least eight cards in length. It's very hard to bid over three clubs with only a six-count! But West was the one with short clubs and he could have made a takeout double of three clubs. Even though this was technically in the direct seat, he would really have been 'balancing', since three clubs was a sign-off. Most players will understandably find it unpalatable to enter the auction with West's hand, but the concept is still worth noting.

2) SCRAMBLING 2NT

As you can imagine, we end up making a lot of takeout doubles when the opponents **B**id **A**nd **R**aise a major. It's very important for us to 'scramble' into our best fit (hopefully an eight-carder!).

When they've bid and raised a suit, and we double (whether in direct or balancing seat), we have a simple rule: **We can't play in two notrump**.

For one thing, we'd never want to play in two notrump. They have an eight-card-fit suit that they're going to lead. We won't enjoy trying to take eight tricks when they have at least half the deck and are starting out by leading their best suit (see Chapter Seven, 'Notrump and the LAW').

So, after partner's takeout double we define two notrump as *Scrambling*, meaning, 'Partner, I'm not sure what to bid.' We usually make this call when we have no standout suit to bid. Often, we'll have 4-4 in two suits and not want to pick one. Sometimes we'll have four small cards in their suit, and three in every other suit.

Here are some examples of Scrambling 2NT after partner has balanced. In each case the auction has gone:

LHO	Partner	RHO	You
1♠	pass	2♠	pass
pass	dbl	pass	2NT

1)   ♠ 7 5 4 3 ♡ K 4 2 ◇ A 4 3 ♣ Q 5 2

Not fun - but we certainly can't pass two spades doubled, and we don't want to guess which three-card suit to bid. Most players bid three hearts in this situation on the assumption that partner will have four cards in the other major. We bid two notrump asking partner to choose a suit. It's like making a responsive double to his takeout double. Maybe he'll have a five-card suit — he'd double two spades with the following shapes: 1-5-4-3, 1-4-5-3, or 1-4-3-5. Why should we guess which suit to bid and risk playing in a 3-3 fit, instead of a 4-3 or 5-3 fit?

2)   ♠ J 4 3 ♡ Q 2 ◇ K 10 5 2 ♣ K 6 5 4

Delighted to bid two notrump — why risk picking partner's three-card minor? He'll bid his cheapest four-card suit, and we'll avoid playing in a 4-3 fit. We would, however, bid three clubs with:

        ♠ J 4 3 ♡ Q 2 ◇ J 6 4 3 ♣ K Q J 4

in an attempt to get a club lead against an eventual contract of three spades.

3)   ♠ Q 5 2 ♡ Q 7 5 ◇ Q J 3 ♣ A 6 4 3

No reason to bid three clubs. Bid Scrambling 2NT and partner will bid his cheapest four-card suit. If he has four clubs, we'll get to clubs. If he has only three clubs then he'll bid a red suit. Maybe he's 2-3-5-3, or 1-4-5-3. Why should we insist on playing in clubs when we'll get there anyway (if it's right) by starting with two notrump?

One further advantage of Scrambling 2NT is that it makes things easier for the takeout doubler himself. Say you have doubled after **1♠ - pass - 2♠** with

♠ 5 ♡ Q J 10 4 ◇ K Q J 9 2 ♣ A 5 4

You're not playing Scrambling 2NT and your partner bids three clubs. Should you pass, or pull to three diamonds, asking partner to choose between the two red suits? This is the auction so far:

LHO	Partner	RHO	You
1♠	pass	2♠	dbl
pass	3♣	pass	??

If you pass, you'll be very unhappy if partner's three-club bid was based on any of the following shapes: 3-3-3-4, 4-1-4-4, 3-2-4-4, 4-3-3-3, etc. You'd be in a six- or seven-card club fit when you had an 8+ card fit available in diamonds! What if you correct to three diamonds, though, and partner really had a five-card club suit? If he held 4-2-2-5 or 4-3-1-5 shape, you'd be missing your eight-card club fit in favor of a seven-card red-suit fit! Playing Scrambling 2NT, you have an easy pass over three clubs. You know partner really has clubs, and rarely fewer than five of them. If he had only four he'd bid two notrump, unless his shape was something like 4-3-2-4.

We also play Scrambling 2NT in other auctions where they haven't bid and raised — but that requires a lot of partnership discussion.

3) 'SUPER' UNUSUAL 2NT

Most people play Unusual 2NT to show the two lowest unbid suits. Its normal application is a jump over the opponents' opening bid. We also play Unusual 2NT after they've bid and raised. However, it shows any two suits — not necessarily the two lowest. What if the bidding goes **1♠ - pass - 2♠** and you hold

♠ 3 ♡ A 10 9 4 3 ◇ 5 2 ♣ A 10 9 8 3

You'd hate to guess which suit to 'balance' with. If you make a takeout double, you know that your dumb ol' partner will bid three diamonds.

So, we bid two notrump saying: 'Partner, I have two suits — bid accordingly'. If partner has 4-1-5-3 shape he'll start out with three clubs in response, knowing that if you have red suits you'll convert to three diamonds. If clubs is one of your suits you'll pass. Yes, if you have clubs and diamonds you'll be in your eight-card fit instead of your ten-card fit — but the object of getting into these auctions is simply to find any fit.

Playing two notrump equals any two suits, and responding cautiously, we are able to sneak into the auction safely, confident that we'll be able to land in a playable trump suit.

4) GOOD-BAD 2NT

This highly useful concept can best be explained with an example. Say you open the bidding with one heart, holding

♠ 4 3   ♡ A K 5 4 2   ◇ 4   ♣ K J 10 6 3

Your partner responds one notrump and your right-hand opponent bids two spades. Despite your mere 11 high-card points you'd love to bid three clubs. After all, you know the opponents have at least eight spades (partner denied four when he bid one notrump), so you can't leave them at the two-level.

The problem with bidding three clubs is that you would also have to bid three clubs with a 17-count! How does partner know if you're just competing, or if you really have a good hand? This kind of problem comes up all the time — you'd love to bid, but you're afraid to mislead partner about the strength of your hand.

We solve this problem with Good-Bad 2NT, a variation of the Lebensohl convention. It enables us to compete to the three-level in a very effective manner. Here is the rule:

> In a competitive auction, when RHO makes any two-level call, our 2NT bid is not natural. It shows a desire to compete to the three-level, and requests that partner bid three clubs, after which the 2NT bidder shows his suit.

If the suit is clubs the two-notrump bidder can pass the forced three-club bid. Bidding directly on the three-level (without relaying first with two notrump) shows extras.

Here are examples illustrating the usefulness of Good-Bad 2NT:

West	North	East	You
			1♡
1♠	1NT	2♠	??

♠ 4 2   ♡ A K J 10 5 4 2   ◊ K 6 4   ♣ 3

An easy two-notrump bid — partner won't play you for an 18-count when you pull his three-club relay to three hearts. If you held

♠ K 2   ♡ A K J 10 5 4 2   ◊ K 6 4   ♣ 3

you would bid three hearts directly.

West	North	East	You
1♡	2◊	2♡	??

♠ K 4 2   ♡ A 4 3   ◊ Q 10 9 6   ♣ 6 5 4

Here, you can bid three diamonds and partner will know that you have a good three-diamond raise. If you held only

♠ 5 4 2   ♡ A 4 3   ◊ Q 10 5 2   ♣ 6 5 4

you would bid two notrump, forcing partner to bid three clubs. Now when you correct to three diamonds, partner will know that you have a minimum raise.

West	North	East	You
			1♡
2♣	pass	2♠	??

♠ 2   ♡ A K Q 6 4   ◊ A K J 6 2   ♣ 3 2

Bid three diamonds and partner will know that you have a good hand (you didn't bid two notrump first). If instead, you held

♠ 2   ♡ A 6 5 3 2   ◊ A K J 6 2   ♣ 3 2

you'd bid two notrump, then three diamonds after partner's forced three-club bid.

West	North	East	You
			1◇
1♠	dbl	2♠	??

♠ 3 2 ♡ K J 10 4 ◇ A K 7 6 2 ♣ 3 2

In Standard, you'd feel uncomfortable bidding a free three hearts. But you can't leave the opponents in their eight-card fit at the two-level. Playing Good-Bad 2NT, you bid two notrump followed by three hearts, to let partner know that you have a minimum.

The number of auctions in which this two-notrump option is available is staggering. However, we've found that in some situations it doesn't make sense to play it. Any serious partnership should take a little time to discuss when it should or should not apply. Some of the exceptions, discussed in *Better Bidding With Bergen*, are the following:

1) When two notrump would clearly be Unusual.
2) When either side has opened one notrump.
3) When the opponents have opened with a big club.
4) When the opponents make a penalty double.
5) When we have already found a fit.
6) When we are already in a game forcing auction.

Even if you choose not to discuss exceptions, you do have to use a little common sense. Let's say your partner opens one diamond, they bid one heart, and you make a negative double holding

♠ A 5 4 2 ♡ A 3 ◇ 7 5 4 ♣ A J 5 2

They raise to two hearts and your partner bids 2NT Good-Bad. He's probably got a weak three-club bid or a weak three-diamond bid. You certainly can't afford to bid three clubs since he will pass if he has clubs! So, you simply bid three hearts and partner will know you have a good hand.

Look how easy it becomes to handle situations like the following: You hold

♠ A 4 ♡ A 6 5 3 ◇ J 10 4 2 ♣ 5 4 3

You	LHO	Partner	RHO
		1◇	1♠
dbl	2♠	3♡	pass
??			

You made a negative double and heard partner bid three hearts over their raise to two spades. You know that partner has a good hand since he didn't bid two notrump. So, you can comfortably raise to game. If partner held only

♠ K 2 ♡ K Q 7 2 ◇ K Q 5 3 ♣ J 6 2

he would not have bid a direct three hearts. He would have started with two notrump, and you would bid three diamonds (no reason to bid three clubs since, if he has diamonds and clubs, you would prefer to play in diamonds). Then, when he bids three hearts, you can pass without worrying that you're missing a game.

Using Good-Bad 2NT, you will be able to compete quite effectively when the opponents find their fit on the two-level — and that's what the LAW wants you to do! You certainly will not suffer from the lack of a natural two-notrump bid — it's not a bid you really need. Telling partner whether you have a *good* or a *bad* three-level bid is a much more useful piece of information to convey.

5) AGGRESSIVE MINOR-SUIT RAISES

Aggressively raising minor-suit openings, in certain situations, is another way to keep the opponents from playing at their proper LAW level. This is a difficult concept because of the ambiguous length promised by one-club and one-diamond openings. A full discussion of such raises can be found in *Better Bidding With Bergen*, but as far as the LAW is concerned, there is one important idea to be presented here.

Say your partner opens one diamond and you are looking at

♠ K 4 2 ♡ 2 ◇ J 5 4 3 ♣ J 6 5 4 2

Your partner's one-diamond opening bid usually shows at least a four-card suit, so your side probably has at least eight diamonds. More importantly, let's think about how many hearts the opponents have. We'll rule out the extremely rare possibility that partner has six diamonds and five hearts. He's expected to have at most four hearts which means that we have at most five hearts between us. So, the opponents have at least an eight-card fit in hearts.

If we give them room, they will certainly find hearts. Why should we let them? Let's bid a preemptive three diamonds right away. Whether they pass, overcall, or double one diamond, we play that the jump-raise is preemptive. We have other methods (Inverted Minors are what most people use) to show a forcing raise when they don't overcall, and we can cuebid if they do.

Anytime you have a singleton in a major, and your partner opens the bidding with one-of-a-minor, a little bell should go off in your head. You immediately know that the opponents are going to be 'LAW satisfied' if they get to two-of-their-major. If you have a weak hand, you want to strain to immediately get the bidding past two-of-their-major, even if you have to lie a little bit about your hand.

Let's assume that you are playing matchpoints with nobody vulnerable, and your partner has opened one club. We would jump to three clubs after a one-heart overcall on all of the following hands:

LHO	Partner	RHO	You
	1♣	1♡	??

♠ 4 3   ♡ 5 4 3   ◇ 3 2   ♣ J 7 6 5 4 3

An easy preempt to at least three clubs — this doesn't promise any points.

♠ 5 4 3   ♡ 5 4 3   ◇ 3 2   ♣ K J 5 4 3

Still an easy three-club bid. Granted, partner could have only three clubs, but he will usually have four. Besides, we don't mind getting to the three-level with eight trumps if there is a good chance that the opponents have a fit.

♠ 6 5 4 3   ♡ 4 3   ◇ K 3   ♣ Q J 5 4 3

Bid three clubs. Yes, we could bid spades (or make a negative double of one heart), but it's much more important to get the bidding past the two-heart-level!

♠ 5 4 3   ♡ 3   ◇ J 10 6 5 4   ♣ Q J 4 3

We would risk a three-club bid — even though we'd love to have another club. The opponents are guaranteed to have eight hearts, so desperate measures are called for.

♠ 5 4 3   ♡ 3   ◇ Q J 5 4   ♣ K J 5 4 3

This is a bit heavy for a preemptive raise, but we'd do it anyway. It's just too important to quickly get past two hearts and make it tougher for LHO.

On all of the above hands we would make the same jump to three clubs over a takeout double.

Jumping directly to three or four of your suit makes things awfully tough for the opponents, and they will often do the wrong thing. Be extra aggressive when your hand tells you that they must have an eight-card major-suit fit. Don't worry about it if you get a bad result every now and then — you'll get five good ones for every bad one, because the opponents will be unable to consistently guess right when deprived of their bidding space.

A Word of Warning

All of the methods presented in this chapter are aids for getting the opponents out of their two-level fit. But we must be cautious. Balancing, to get the opponents off the two-level, is sometimes a risky proposition. Following are some auctions where there is no guarantee of an eight-card fit for the opponents:

Opener	Responder
1♢	1♡
2♡	

Many players correctly raise one-of-a-major with only three-card support.

Opener	Responder
1♠	1NT
2♣	2♠

Responder is just giving a preference and may have only two-card support.

Opener	Responder
1♡	1♠
2♣	2♡

Responder will often have two-card support.

Opener	Responder
1♡	1NT
2♡	pass

Responder could be void!

The auctions that you especially want to bid over are those where a) they open and raise a major, or b) they overcall and raise. But one further word of caution — look at this auction:

Opener	Partner	Responder	You
1♡	pass	2♡	pass
pass	2♠	3♡	??

Be very careful about hanging partner for balancing. Let's say you are looking at:

♠ K54 ♡ A32 ◇ A543 ♣ 643

Are you tempted to bid three spades? Don't even think about it! The idea was to get them out of two hearts. Be thankful that partner did just that. You should know by now that this is a LAW situation. There rate to be only 16 trumps, and we shouldn't bid three-over-three.

Try to train yourself always to think about the LAW in any competitive auction. Suppose you are dealt

♠ A42 ♡ A2 ◇ K10964 ♣ J52

and open the bidding one diamond. You're playing matchpoints and nobody is vulnerable. Your partner responds one notrump which your RHO doubles. You pass and hear LHO's two-heart bid come back around to you. This has been the auction so far:

You	LHO	Partner	RHO
1◇	pass	1NT	dbl
pass	2♡	pass	pass
??			

This situation is tailor-made for the LAW. Partner's one notrump denied a four-card major, so the opponents must have at least an eight-card heart fit. You also know that partner, who has at most 3-3 in the majors, must have at least seven cards in the minors. If he has three diamonds and four clubs, your side has an eight-card diamond fit. If he has two diamonds and five clubs, then your side has an eight-card club fit. So, you know that both sides have at least an eight-card fit, and you know that passing two hearts cannot possibly get you a good result. As to *what* to bid ... that's a story for another book.

This concludes our discussion of ways to keep the opponents from playing at their proper LAW level. All of the methods in this chapter dealt with the most important competitive-level as far as the LAW is concerned — the two-level. Getting the opponents off the two-level when they have eight trumps is extremely productive, because we can do that without getting too high ourselves. When the opponents are at the three- or four-level (even if they have nine or ten trumps), it is not as easy to disturb them. Sometimes we have to concede them the higher levels because there will not be enough Total Trumps to compete. The next chapter examines the higher levels in more detail.

CHAPTER REVIEW

- When the opponents stop at the two-level with eight trumps they are in a good position. Therefore, we should try very hard not to let them play there.

- Some of the methods we use for keeping the opponents from playing on the two-level are:

  1) OBAR BIDS — Balancing In Direct Seat

  2) Scrambling 2NT to say 'pick a suit partner'

  3) 'Super' Unusual 2NT as takeout for any two suits

  4) Good-Bad 2NT, to be able to compete with minimum hands

  5) Aggressive minor-suit raises, to get quickly past two-of-their-major

- Be wary of competing against auctions that don't guarantee an eight-card fit.

- Don't hang partner for balancing.

1) The auction has gone:

LHO	Partner	RHO	You
		1♡	pass
2♡	pass	pass	??

  a) Why should you balance?

  b) What's the lowest number of Total Tricks there can be?

  c) What's the lowest number of Total Tricks there are likely to be?

  d) Is vulnerability or form of scoring relevant?

2) The auction has been:

LHO	Partner	RHO	You
1♠	pass	2♠	??

  You hold

  ♠ x x   ♡ x x   ◊ K x x   ♣ K J 10 9 8 x

Neither side is vulnerable. What should you do and why?

3) With neither vulnerable the bidding has been:

LHO	Partner	RHO	You
1♠	pass	2♠	pass
pass	dbl	pass	??

What should you do with:

  a) ♠ K x x x   ♡ x   ◊ Q x x x   ♣ Q J x x

  b) ♠ Q x x   ♡ K x x x   ◊ K x x x   ♣ x x

  c) ♠ A x x x   ♡ Q x x   ◊ Q x x   ♣ J x x

  d) ♠ K x x x   ♡ x x   ◊ Q x x x x   ♣ x x

4) At favorable vulnerability the auction has gone:

LHO	Partner	RHO	You
1♠	pass	2♠	??

What's your action with

♠ A x ♡ K J 10 x x ◊ x ♣ Q J 9 x x

5) With nobody vulnerable the auction has gone:

RHO	Partner	LHO	You
			1◊
1♠	dbl	2♠	??

What should you do with each of the following?

a) ♠ A x ♡ A x ◊ Q J 10 9 8 7 ♣ x x x

b) ♠ x x x x ♡ A Q ◊ A K J 9 x x ♣ x

c) ♠ A x x ♡ Q J 10 8 ◊ Q J 10 8 ♣ K x

d) ♠ K x x ♡ K x x ◊ Q J 10 8 ♣ A x x

6) West has a 2-3-4-4 13-count. On which of the following auctions do North-South rate to have an eight-card fit in one of the majors?

West	North	East	South
1♣	1♠	dbl	2♠

West	North	East	South
1♣	pass	1NT	dbl

West	North	East	South
1◊	dbl	2◊	2♡

West	North	East	South
1◊	1♡	1NT	2♠

7) Both sides are vulnerable at IMPs. What action do you take?

a)
LHO	Partner	RHO	You
	1NT[1]	2◊[2]	??

1. 12-14.
2. Spades and another suit.

♠ J 9 6 4 ♡ K 10 8 5 ◊ 10 7 3 ♣ K 3

b)

	LHO	Partner	RHO	You
		2♣[1]	pass	pass
	dbl	redbl	2♡	??

1. Precision (11-15 HCP, 6+ clubs).

♠ J 7 3 2   ♡ 9   ◊ K 9 8 7 5 4   ♣ Q 2

CHAPTER 5   ANSWERS

1) **a)** Because they have eight trumps and are therefore 'LAW sufficient' at the two-level.

   b) 15. Only if your side has exactly five hearts, seven spades, seven diamonds, and seven clubs for its 26 cards.

   c) 16. Because the scenario described in 1(b) is statistically not going to occur often. Your side will normally have at least an eight-card fit.

   d) Yes, but only as a secondary consideration. When vulnerable against nonvulnerable opponents, a small degree of conservatism is prudent.

2) Bid three clubs. Balance In Direct Seat. Not only does it get them out of two spades, but you can be sure that clubs is a good suit to compete in (you don't want partner to balance with three-of-a-red-suit). Also, it's a good lead-directing bid. Your lack of high-card points should not deter you.

3) **a)** Bid two notrump. Don't guess which minor to bid — you might hit a three-card suit. Let partner bid his cheaper four-card minor so that you'll be guaranteed to find at least an eight-card fit.

   b) Bid two notrump. Again, don't guess which suit to bid. If partner bids three diamonds — pass. Don't worry about getting to the major. The idea is just to get in safely and get them out of two spades. If partner bids three clubs, you can now bid three diamonds to give him a choice between diamonds and hearts.

- c) Bid two notrump. Not very pretty, but who wants to guess which three-card suit to pick? Maybe partner will have a five-card suit to bid over two notrump. Besides, let's let partner play this one!

- d) Bid three diamonds. Partner will be pretty sure that we have five of them from our failure to bid two notrump.

4) Bid two notrump, which shows any two suits. Partner will be careful to respond three clubs with 3-2-5-3 shape since he'll bid the cheapest suit he can stand. If you double (which would show all three suits) partner could ruin everything by bidding three diamonds.

5) a) Bid two notrump intending to convert three clubs to three diamonds.

- b) Bid a direct three diamonds to show your extras.

- c) Bid two notrump and convert three clubs to three hearts.

- d) Pass. Yes, they have eight spades, but there is no convenient bid to make. Leave it up to partner who will also assume that they have eight spades.

6) All of them. Don't let them play there!

7) a) Pass. There is no indication they have an eight-card fit.

- b) Three clubs. They have eight hearts and we must get them off the two-level.

DOUBLE TROUBLE

CHAPTER 6

Harassment. Obstruction. Interference. Why won't those *$#@&!% opponents stay out of our auctions?! How can we bid properly when we're constantly put to a guess at a high-level?

As usual, we'll rely on the Law of Total Tricks.

Decisions at the Four-Level

Suppose the opponents open the bidding with four-of-a-major, and your partner doubles. The first question is, what does the double show? There are two ways of playing it. One is penalty-oriented — usually showing about the strength of a strong notrump with at least two cards in the suit opened. The second way is to play it as more takeout-oriented, usually showing shortness in the suit that was opened. There is no *right* way to play the double. Some partnerships play it one way over four hearts, but differently over four spades. The important thing is to have a partnership agreement as to which way you are playing it.

No matter how you define double (takeout or penalty), there has to be a bit of an overlap between the two treatments. Playing penalty doubles you'd certainly double a four-spade opening if you held

♠ K ♡ A K 5 ◇ A Q 6 2 ♣ A 7 5 3 2

What else could you do? Playing takeout doubles you'd want to double a four-heart opening if you held

♠ A 7 5 2 ♡ A 5 3 ◇ A 6 2 ♣ A 6 2

So, in rare cases, a penalty double could have as little as one trump, while a takeout double could have as many as three!

If you are playing the double as penalty-oriented, then responding to it is fairly easy. Knowing that your partner normally has at least two trumps, and a relatively balanced hand, makes it easy to apply the Law of Total Tricks. As you might imagine, your conclusion will almost always be to pass the double.

Opponents open four spades

Let's say that with neither vulnerable the opponents open four spades and your partner doubles for penalty. Let's look at some typical hands:

♠ 6 5 ♡ K 10 9 3 ◇ Q 7 4 2 ♣ K 9 3

They have at most nine trumps (we're assuming 2+ spades for partner) and we don't rate to have more than eight. That makes at most 17 and, if you made it through Chapter Two, you'll pass without much difficulty.

♠ J 4 ♡ A 9 8 5 3 ◇ K 9 8 ♣ Q 8 7

Still an easy pass, though it might tempt some people. Using the LAW, we figure nine trumps for them (partner rates to have two or three) and eight or nine for us (again assuming partner has at most four in one of our suits) for a total of 17 or 18. If we have 11 tricks, they have only six or seven.

The theme is clear. Unless there are an unusually large number of trumps (at least 20!), don't consider pulling a penalty double of four spades.

Opponents open four hearts

If the opening bid were four hearts instead, and the responder to the (penalty) double had a lot of spades, bidding might be a possibility:

♠ A 8 6 4 ♡ Q 9 2 ◇ K 8 7 2 ♣ K 6

They probably have eight hearts (we're still assuming partner has two), and we probably have seven or eight spades (generously assigning partner three or four for his 'strong notrump' type of hand). Let's take the averages and call it 8 + 7½ or 15½. If we can make ten tricks in spades (+420), they will have only five or six (+1100 or +800) in four hearts. We should pass.

♠ A Q 8 7 4 3 ♡ 8 ◇ A 4 3 ♣ 7 5 2

Now they have at least nine or ten hearts. We have eight, nine, or ten spades for an expectancy of nine, so the total is almost 19 tricks. Finally, we have an example of a hand that should bid over the double. With 19 tricks, how can we be wrong?

As you can see, it takes an extreme distribution in order for it to be right to pull a penalty double of a four-of-a-major opening bid.

Now, let's think about the decision after a takeout double. We will make the assumption that partner's average holding in their suit for a takeout double is a singleton. Yes, he could have a void or a doubleton, but his most likely (and average) number is one. When we contemplate action over his takeout double, we can also expect that, on balance, he will have four-card support for our suit(s). (Again, this is an average — three or five-card length is certainly a possibility.)

With this in mind, let's again assume that nobody is vulnerable; they open four hearts, and partner makes a takeout double. To solve each problem, simply picture partner with 4-1-4-4 distribution.

♠ K 5 4 3 ♡ K 4 3 ◊ A 4 2 ♣ K 8 7

Easy for LAW users. We're estimating that partner has one heart and four of everything else. So, they have nine hearts and we have eight spades for a total of 17 trumps. If we have ten tricks, for +420 then they will have only seven tricks for +500. And, of course, if we have fewer than ten tricks we definitely want to pass.

♠ A Q 4 3 2 ♡ 3 2 ◊ 8 7 6 4 ♣ Q 4

Here, instincts and the LAW lead to the same conclusion. We assume ten hearts for them, nine spades for us — 19 tricks. Whether the tricks are split 10-9 (either way), or even 11-8 (either way), we want to bid four spades.

♠ A 8 7 ♡ 3 2 ◊ K 6 4 2 ♣ K 5 3 2

Again, no problem for LAW followers. They have ten, we have eight — for a total of 18. If we can make five-of-a-minor (11 tricks), then they are going for 500 (seven tricks). pass is correct. If you're not convinced, take a look at the full deal (from a Chatham, New Jersey Sectional):

```
Neither Vul.              ♠ K Q 9 5
Dealer West               ♡ A
                          ◊ Q J 8 5
                          ♣ Q J 7 6
        ♠ J 10 3          ┌─────────┐      ♠ 6 4 2
        ♡ K Q J 10 9 7 6  │   N     │      ♡ 8 5 4
        ◊ 3               │ W     E │      ◊ A 10 9 7
        ♣ 10 9            │   S     │      ♣ A 8 4
                          └─────────┘
                          ♠ A 8 7
                          ♡ 3 2
                          ◊ K 6 4 2
                          ♣ K 5 3 2
```

In the Open Pairs, some of the Wests chose to open with four hearts. North doubled, and South had to decide what to do. Those who pulled the double wound up going minus in five-of-a-minor. There were only 18 trumps — not enough tricks to warrant competing to the five-level. The Souths who followed the LAW and passed the double were rewarded with a good score.

When deciding whether or not to take out a double of four-of-a-major, try to estimate the number of trumps. The combination of reasonable estimating and judicious LAW usage will lead you to the right decision much more often than guessing or trying to use 'judgment'.

In our discussion of taking out doubles at the four-level, we have limited ourselves so far to an opening bid of four-of-a-major. Here's a deal from the 1989 Spingold in Chicago, which involved a four-level responsive double:

N-S Vul.
Dealer West

```
                    ♠ K 10 9 4
                    ♡ A J 4
                    ◇ K 9 7 4
                    ♣ 3 2
  ♠ J 7 6          ┌──────────┐        ♠ 5 3 2
  ♡ 10 9 6 2       │    N     │        ♡ 8 5
  ◇ A Q 10       W │          │ E      ◇ J 8
  ♣ A Q 6          │    S     │        ♣ K J 10 9 8 7
                   └──────────┘
                    ♠ A Q 8
                    ♡ K Q 7 3
                    ◇ 6 5 3 2
                    ♣ 5 4
```

In one semi-final match this was the auction:

West	North	East	South
Kantar	*Cayne*	*Sontag*	*Burger*
1♣	dbl	4♣	dbl
pass	4◇	pass	4♡
pass	4♠	all pass	

Four-of-a-major for North-South is doomed, since there are two losers in each minor. Here, Burger did well to make a responsive double of four clubs, instead of bidding four hearts. Cayne should have known there were not nearly enough trumps to bid 'four-over-four,' and should have passed the double for an easy +500.

Listed below are some frequently occurring auctions where we will have to decide what to do over a double of a four-level preempt which was not the opening bid. These auctions cause headaches for experienced players and beginners alike. The problems are much easier to solve when using the LAW. Let's 'deal' ourselves a few hands and see what decisions we can make on the above auctions. We'll assume that both sides are vulnerable at matchpoints.

LHO	Partner	RHO	You
		1♡	pass
4♡	dbl	pass	??

♠ A 8 7 6   ♡ 3   ◇ Q 5 4 3 2   ♣ K 6 5

We should assume that they have at least nine, and quite likely ten hearts. Partner will more often than not have four spades, so there are probably 18 trumps. Defending could be right (if each side has exactly nine tricks), but bidding four spades will be right if either side can make ten tricks. We should bid four spades. (If it turns out that there were only 17 trumps, we've probably done the wrong thing!)

LHO	Partner	RHO	You
		pass	1◇
4♡	dbl	pass	??

♠ K 6 5   ♡ 4 2   ◇ A Q J 10 8   ♣ K J 3

The modern day treatment of partner's double in this auction is that it shows 'cards.' It should not be played as a trump stack because that's a highly unlikely occurrence. It tends to show about nine or more high-card points and covers a wide range of hands. We can only begin to guess how many trumps there are, but let's try. The four-heart bidder rates to have seven or eight hearts. We expect that everyone else at the table has approximately a doubleton, and someone probably has a singleton. At any rate, partner probably has one or two, giving them nine or ten. As to our fit, we might have nine diamonds, but it's likely that our best fit is no longer than eight cards. That makes 9½ + 8, or a total of 17½ trumps. If we were to bid five diamonds, we know the LAW would not be with us. If we have 11 tricks, they have only six or seven! If we bid four spades hoping partner has a four-card suit, that would give us only seven trumps, for a total of only 16 or 17. The LAW doesn't suggest bidding four spades either. So passing the double is clearly indicated.

LHO	Partner	RHO	You
		3♡	dbl
4♡	dbl	pass	??

♠ K 6 5 ♡ 4 2 ◇ A Q J 10 8 ♣ K J 3

Let's say we had the same hand as the previous example, and heard this auction instead. We chose to double the three-heart opening (a bit aggressively) and partner doubled their raise to four hearts. Again, this double is played by most people as card-showing. In deciding what to do, we can use the exact same reasoning as before: 'pass' is the only choice.

LHO	Partner	RHO	You
pass	1◇	4♡	pass
pass	dbl	pass	??

♠ K 8 7 6 ♡ J 10 4 2 ◇ 8 3 ♣ Q 4 3

We have to decide whether or not to pull partner's double. He's opened one diamond, and doubled their four-heart overcall. This double shows extras but says nothing about hearts. Our heart length suggests that partner is likely to have only one or two; that gives them eight or nine hearts. We might have eight spades which would make 16 or 17 trumps. Obviously, 17 tricks does not suggest pulling the double. Even if we can make four spades (ten tricks), we rate to get 800 (seven tricks) by passing.

LHO	Partner	RHO	You
		2♡	2♠
4♡	dbl	pass	??

♠ K Q J 10 8 5 3 ♡ 2 ◇ A J 10 ♣ 5 3

This time, we overcalled their weak two-heart bid with two spades, and partner doubled their raise to four hearts. Again, this double should simply show 'cards.' Well, it seems like a bit of a stab to count trumps — but let's try. They rate to have nine

or ten hearts. Partner rates to have one, two, or three spades —
so let's call it two. They have 9½ and we have 9, for a total of 18½.
Chapters Three and Nine suggest that we might adjust upwards
for a long suit with great interiors, along with a lack of minor
honors and a potential double-fit (if partner is say, 2-3-5-3). All
of these factors cause us to assume there are at least 19 trumps,
and that means we should bid four spades. If there are 19
trumps, somebody will be able to take at least ten tricks.

The following deal, from the 1982 World Open Pairs
Championship in Biarritz, illustrates quite clearly the type of
decision that 'experts' often get wrong:

Both Vul.
Dealer West

```
                    ♠ K J 8
                    ♡ A Q 10 7
                    ◇ A Q 6
                    ♣ J 10 5
  ♠ A 10 7 6 4 3   ┌─────────┐   ♠ 5
  ♡ K J 6 4        │    N    │   ♡ 9
  ◇ J 10 7         │ W     E │   ◇ 5 4 3 2
  ♣ —              │    S    │   ♣ A Q 9 8 7 4 2
                   └─────────┘
                    ♠ Q 9 2
                    ♡ 8 5 3 2
                    ◇ K 9 8
                    ♣ K 6 3
```

West	North	East	South
Kokish	*Branco*	*Nagy*	*Cintra*
pass	1♣[1]	4♣	dbl
pass	4♡	all pass	

1. Strong, artificial.

West passed, and North opened with a strong club. The East
player, Canadian Peter Nagy, jumped to four clubs preemptively, and South doubled to show 'high cards'. North now made a
fatal decision which any LAW follower would easily avoid. He
bid four hearts (and was fortunate to go down only one trick).
Yes, he was unlucky that his partner had as many as three clubs,
but on the other hand, he was fortunate to find four-card heart
support.

What would his thinking have been if he had used the LAW?
He'd expect East to hold seven or eight clubs. He's looking at

three clubs, which leaves two or three clubs between his partner and the preemptor's partner. So, the preemptor's partner rates to have one or two clubs. Therefore the opponents have seven or eight clubs in one hand opposite one or two clubs in the other hand (7½ + 1½), for an expectancy of nine clubs. How many hearts does the doubler rate to have? Certainly not too many, or he would have bid four hearts on his own. Probably not too few, or he would have been bidding spades or diamonds. So he should assume that partner has three or four hearts (3½), making 7½ for his side. That's a total of 9 + 7½, or 16½ Total Trumps.

By now you probably realize that 16 or 17 trumps aren't even close to being enough to bid four-over-four. If you make ten or eleven tricks in hearts, they'd be going for 800 or 1100!

On the actual deal there were only 15 trumps and, obviously, neither side can take many tricks. West should have applied a 'four-trump double' (see Chapter Eight) — but it was North who needed to read all the chapters in this book!

The following deal appeared in Alan Truscott's *Sunday New York Times* bridge column in May 1984. It helped Marty Bergen and me win the prestigious Cavendish Pairs that year:

N-S Vul.
Dealer East

```
                    ♠ A 9 3
                    ♡ K 9 7 5
                    ◇ 9
                    ♣ A K 8 7 4
    ♠ K J 5 2                          ♠ 10 6
    ♡ A Q 10 6 2      N                ♡ J 4 3
    ◇ 5 2          W       E           ◇ K J 10 8 7 4 3
    ♣ Q 5             S                ♣ 3
                    ♠ Q 8 7 4
                    ♡ 8
                    ◇ A Q 6
                    ♣ J 10 9 6 2
```

West	North	East	South
		4◇	pass
pass	dbl	pass	4♠
dbl	pass	pass	4NT
dbl	all pass		

West doubled four spades, and then doubled the runout to four notrump. South won the diamond lead and crossed to dummy in clubs, in order to lead the spade three to his eight and West's jack. Declarer eventually led the spade queen to pin East's ten. West didn't cover, but declarer led a heart towards his king for his tenth trick and scored +810. (A heart lead might have defeated the contract.)

That intra-finesse in spades was quite nice, but this is not a book on card play. It's a book on the Law of Total Tricks, and sadly to say, the author of this book was South in the diagram! Suffice to say that I didn't know as much about the LAW in 1984 as I do now, or I would have passed four diamonds doubled and collected 500. My hand should have screamed to me that there were not enough Total Trumps to do anything other than defend! (Yes, with partner having five clubs and only one diamond, a five-club bid would have yielded +600, but it's much better, in the long run, to take a sure +300 or +500, than sometimes to score 600 or 620, but often go –100.*

It's some consolation to me that the great French player, Christian Mari, erred in a similar situation in the 1975 World Championships in Bermuda. In the semifinals against the United States, he held the following cards:

♠ Q J 3 2   ♡ Q 10 8   ◇ A 5   ♣ 9 8 7 3

With nobody vulnerable, his LHO opened the bidding with four diamonds, which was doubled. Mari did what most players would do — he bid four spades, and was defeated one trick. His partner was 4-4-1-4, and thus it's no surprise that the winning action was to pass. Even though there were more trumps than there might have been (partner could have had more diamonds, or fewer spades), there still were only nine tricks for each side.

See if you can apply the LAW to the following four-level decision. Nobody is vulnerable and you are holding

♠ A K 6 4 2   ♡ K 6 3   ◇ J   ♣ A 5 4 2

You open the bidding with one spade and partner makes a negative double of the opponent's two-diamond overcall. Your RHO jumps preemptively to four diamonds:

---

* The Cavendish pairs is scored by IMPs across the field.

You	LHO	Partner	RHO
1♠	2◇	dbl	4◇
??			

You have too good a hand to pass, so your choices lie between double, four hearts, and five clubs. Most experienced players, when given this hand as a problem, bid four hearts. They reason that the 4-3 fit should play quite well with the short hand being able to take diamond ruffs.

If we have a 4-3 heart fit (seven trumps), do we really want to be competing at the four-level? The opponents rate to have nine or ten diamonds. Even if they have ten, there will only be 17 Total Tricks, and if we were to score +420 (ten tricks) in hearts, we'd have +500 (seven tricks) available against four diamonds. Similarly, bidding five clubs makes no sense when you count the trumps and count the tricks. By a process of elimination, our only option is to double four diamonds. This hand, like most other competitive situations, is tailor-made for the LAW!

DECISIONS AT THE THREE-LEVEL

Now let's shift our attention to the three-level. We'll start out, again, with opening preempts by the opponents.

As we have already noted, there is a tendency to preempt on less and less. That should make us want to pass partner's take-out doubles more readily than we would have done in the past. Furthermore, we will see that the Law of Total Tricks suggests passing these takeout doubles much more often than players do in practice.

Let's assume nobody is vulnerable at matchpoints, and your right-hand opponent has opened three hearts. You have passed it around to your partner, who doubles. Let's see what we should do with each of the following hands:

RHO	You	LHO	Partner
3♡	pass	pass	dbl
pass	??		

♠ K 8 7 6   ♡ K J 5 2   ◇ 6 4   ♣ 8 4 2

With better heart spots, most people would pass the double. Using the LAW, you don't need any spots! Assume partner has a typical 4-1-4-4. There will be 8+8 trumps for 16 Total Tricks. If we can make three spades (+140), they can only make seven tricks in hearts (+300). If each side has exactly eight tricks, we still want to pass. Chapter Nine explains why your heart holding argues even more strongly for a pass.

♠ A 4 2   ♡ 10 8 5 3   ◇ A 7 6   ♣ 9 7 5

Years ago, nobody would have dreamed of passing with this hand. Nowadays it has more appeal, because the three-heart bid could be very aggressive. No matter what the year, this is an easy pass using the LAW. Opposite the typical 4-1-4-4, there are only 15 trumps! (If you are considering bidding three notrump, look ahead to Chapter Seven where notrump and the LAW will be discussed. If we have nine tricks in three notrump, they rate to have only six tricks in hearts.)

♠ Q 10 8 7 6   ♡ A 2   ◇ Q 4 3   ♣ 10 8 6

Here, it's a question of bidding three or four spades. There rate to be at least 18 trumps, so we won't consider passing. If you want your partners to keep on balancing, three spades is probably your best action.

♠ K 8 2   ♡ J 4 3   ◇ Q 8 7 5   ♣ A 3 2

This one might make you stop reading this book! Passing feels 'repulsive,' but it is going to be right about nine times in ten! There rate to be at most 16 trumps, and neither side will be able to make any contract at this level. Another problem with pulling the double is that there is nothing appealing to pull to! Three spades, three notrump, and four diamonds are the most likely possibilities. (Not much fun!) Even at IMPs, pass will be the long-run winning action, although you may lose your teammates the one time in ten that you go -530.

It's understandable if it's hard for you to believe that 'pass' is the winning action on this last hand. It's only after years of experience that you can begin to form an opinion as to what this kind of action will accomplish. If you own or have access to a random deal generator, you can experiment with various deals and see the benefits of passing.

Following is a sample printout from a BOREL* simulation of the last problem above. The South hand is fixed as above. East

---

* The late John Lowenthal's computer program for generating bridge deals.

is assigned a three-heart preempt, and North is programmed to have a takeout double. We use the simulation to decide what South should do after the auction has gone **3♡ — pass — pass — dbl — pass**. Next to each deal is a brief analysis of how pass would work out, as opposed to a pull to three spades, three notrump, or four diamonds.

North
♠ Q J 6 5
♡ A K
♢ A 9 3
♣ 10 9 7 6

Bid
3♠ — *probably down 1 or 2 (-50 or –100)*
3NT – *complex – might make (-50 or +400)*
4♢ – *ugh! Minus a lot!*
Pass
3♡ *dbled down at least 2 (+300 or +500)*

West
♠ 10 9 4
♡ 8
♢ K 10 4 2
♣ K Q J 8 5

```
      N
  W       E
      S
```

East
♠ A 7 3
♡ Q 10 9 7 6 5 2
♢ J 6
♣ 4

South
♠ K 8 2
♡ J 4 3
♢ Q 8 7 5
♣ A 3 2

North
♠ A J 7 4
♡ A 6
♢ A 6 4
♣ Q 8 7 4

Bid
3♠ – *down a few (-50, -100 or –150)*
3NT – *interesting possibilities (-50, -100 or +400)*
4♢ – *Not very good! (probably 100)*
Pass
3♡ *dbled — probably down only 1 (+100)*

West
♠ Q 10 9 6 3
♡ 10
♢ K J 10 9
♣ K 10 5

```
      N
  W       E
      S
```

East
♠ 5
♡ K Q 9 8 7 5 2
♢ 3 2
♣ J 9 6

South
♠ K 8 2
♡ J 4 3
♢ Q 8 7 5
♣ A 3 2

```
            North                    Bid
          ♠ A 6 4                    3♠ — How depressing! ( –100)
          ♡ 10                       3NT – Oops! (-150)
          ◇ A K J 4                  4◇ — Probably down 1 (-50)
          ♣ J 10 8 5 4               Pass
                                     3♡ dbled  — down 1 (+100)
West                     East
♠ Q J 10 7 5             ♠ 9 3
♡ A 7          ┌─────┐   ♡ K Q 9 8 6 5 2
◇ 10 6 3       │  N  │   ◇ 9 2
♣ K Q 7        │W   E│   ♣ 9 6
               │  S  │
               └─────┘
            South
          ♠ K 8 2
          ♡ J 4 3
          ◇ Q 8 7 5
          ♣ A 3 2
```

The three deals presented here are pretty much representative of the whole batch. Three hearts doubled was makable on about ten percent of the printout of 100 hands. The most important thing that can be seen from these three examples is that, even if pulling the double is correct, it's very hard to guess right about what to pull to? On the last deal, bidding three spades could land you in a 3-3 fit and bidding three notrump could be totally embarrassing. On the second deal, bidding four diamonds was hardly a success. Even if you can't bring yourself to pass the double on this actual hand, perhaps you can see that the Law of Total Tricks might get you to pass on some hands that you wouldn't have in the past.

Here's a deal from the 1977 World Championships in Manila in a match between the United States and Argentina:

```
N-S Vul.                 ♠ Q 8 6
Dealer West              ♡ K 8 6
                         ◇ A Q 9
                         ♣ 9 7 6 5
      ♠ 9                            ♠ J 10 5 4 2
      ♡ Q J 2      ┌─────┐           ♡ A 10 9 4
      ◇ 10 7 6     │  N  │           ◇ 4 3 2
      ♣ K Q J 10 8 2 │W   E│         ♣ 4
                   │  S  │
                   └─────┘
                         ♠ A K 7 3
                         ♡ 7 5 3
                         ◇ K J 8 5
                         ♣ A 3
```

West	North	East	South
Swanson	*Cabanne*	*Soloway*	*Scanavino*
2♠[1]	pass	3♣	dbl
pass	4♣	pass	4♠
pass	5♠	all pass	

1.   Rubin two-bid.

One possible meaning for the two-spade opening was a three club preempt. East duly bid three clubs, and South entered the auction with a double. At this point, North had a difficult problem. The winning action was to bid three notrump (which makes by throwing East in with spades to lead away from his ace of hearts for the ninth trick), but that was quite an unlikely bid with no club stopper.

North expects to beat three clubs, and has no guarantee that his side has a game. In fact, what does the LAW suggest if his partner has say, 4-4-4-1 distribution? That would mean that the opponents have eight trumps and his side has seven, for a total of 15. So, if North-South can make four-of-a-major (ten tricks), then East-West will be down four (making only five tricks) in three clubs doubled!

Furthermore, why does partner have to be 4-4-4-1? On the actual deal he was 4-3-4-2, and because of the layout of the hearts, three clubs doubled goes down only one trick. East-West have eight tricks in clubs! What does this say about North-South's potential?

Since we are expecting only 15 Total Tricks, we can expect North-South to have only seven tricks! In practice they managed to take eight tricks (mercifully undoubled). North not only failed to pass the double, he fell in love with his four small in clubs and got his side to the five-level! It is worth repeating that four small in the opponents' suit is not always as good as it might seem. It indicates that there are not a lot of Total Trumps, and therefore, not a lot of Total Tricks. It's uncomfortable to pass the double with North's hand, but it's surely the correct action according to the Law of Total Tricks.

The most difficult three-level decisions are not over opening preempts, but are on auctions such as the ones below, which feature preemptive jumps by the opponents. That's the way it is these days. Yes, it's hard to cope with this barrage of interference, but let's try some hands. We'll assume that we are playing matchpoints at unfavorable vulnerability.

We	LHO	Partner	RHO
1◊	3♠	dbl	pass
??			

♠ Q 10 4 2   ♡ A 4 2   ◊ A Q 5 3   ♣ 8 6

We opened one diamond and partner made a negative double of their three-spade jump overcall. Most players would be too uncomfortable with passing, and would bid three notrump. This kind of decision will be better understood after reading Chapter Seven which deals with notrump and the LAW. For now, keep in mind how often it seems that passing these three-level doubles is a possibility. It is certainly the right action on this hand; there are not enough Total Trumps to do anything else.

We	LHO	Partner	RHO
		1♠	3♡
pass	pass	dbl	pass
??			

♠ 4   ♡ 10 7 6 4   ◊ J 7 6 4   ♣ Q 7 6 5

Partner bid one spade and then reopened with a double of their three-heart preempt. I know, I know, you can't stomach the thought of leaving this one in. Can you just think about it? What if partner is 5-2-3-3 with an 18-count. That might get you to pass. Look at all of the following shapes which will produce only 15 trumps: 6-1-3-3, 5-2-4-2, and 5-2-2-4. Even if partner has something like 5-1-4-3 or 5-1-3-4 (and we guess to bid his four-card suit), there will still only be 16 trumps. Yes, you're worried that they'll make three hearts too often, but let's look at the chart:

CHART FOR 16 TOTAL TRICKS			
Unfavorable Vulnerability			
We play four of a minor		They play three hearts doubled	
Our Tricks	Our Score	Their Tricks	Our Score
7	**-300**	9	-530
8	-200	8	**+100**
9	-100	7	**+300**
10	+130	6	**+500**

Look how much better we do by passing the double (right side of chart). And this assumes the maximum number of trumps and that we would pick the right minor! In the case where they make three hearts doubled (-530), we could easily get doubled and go -800 if we bid four-of-a-minor. Even at IMPs, the evidence is overwhelming. You just have to bite the bullet and live with an occasional -530.

We	**LHO**	**Partner**	**RHO**
		pass	1♡
dbl	3♡	dbl	pass
??			

♠ A Q 8 5   ♡ 8 7   ◇ A 4 3 2   ♣ K 9 3

This time we made a takeout double of one heart and partner made a responsive double of their preemptive jump to three hearts. Let's first think about what the responsive double shows. Usually, when we make a takeout double, partner will try to bid a four-card major if he has one. Therefore, a responsive double usually denies a four-card major. However, the higher the level, the less this is true. Put yourself in partner's shoes. He has heard you double and the auction is now up to three hearts. Say he has something like

♠ K 7 4 2   ♡ K 7 5   ◇ K 7 6   ♣ Q 6 2

Should he really bid three spades? Not if he uses the LAW! He'll figure that there are 16 or 17 trumps and will make a responsive double. Now back to our seat. We have heard the responsive double and have to decide what to do. Well, how many spades does partner have? We've just seen that it's possible for him to have four, but on balance he will probably have three. His heart length is probably two, but could be three. If we had to guess his shape we would most likely give him three spades, two hearts, four diamonds, and four clubs. That would mean that there are nine hearts and eight diamonds for 17 Trumps. Should we bid four diamonds? No, just 'follow the chart' for 17 trumps. If we can make four diamonds we'd rather pass three hearts doubled. We can try projecting other shapes for partner, but there aren't too many where the LAW will tell us to do anything other than pass the double. They are not likely to be able to take nine tricks given our side's strength. More than likely, they have eight tricks and we have eight or nine. Pass, and then lead a trump!

We	LHO	Partner	RHO
1♦	1♡	dbl	3♡
pass	pass	dbl	pass
??			

Now let's take the same hand:

♠ A Q 8 5   ♡ 8 7   ◇ A 4 3 2   ♣   ♡ 9 3

with a different auction. We've opened one diamond which was overcalled with one heart. After partner's negative double, the pesky opponents preempted to three hearts. We didn't feel as if we had enough to bid a free three spades and now partner has doubled to show extras. What should we do? This is much different from the last example. Here we are 'guaranteed' to have eight spades — so there is a good chance that there are 17 trumps. But this time we don't have to go to four-of-a-minor — we have an eight-card spade fit. The tricks could easily be split nine for us eight for them. We should bid three spades.

We	LHO	Partner	RHO
		1◇	1♠
dbl	3♠	dbl	pass
??			

♠ Q 5 4   ♡ K J 8 6   ◇ Q 2   ♣ 10 5 4 3

With the same unfavorable vulnerability, let's now consider our last auction. We made a negative double after their one-spade overcall of partner's one-diamond opening bid. They jumped to three spades and partner doubled to show extras. What should we do? To bid three notrump seems wrong since they might run the spades. What about bidding four-of-a-suit? Well, what does partner have? He probably doesn't have four-card length in hearts, or he would have bid four hearts. He's likely to have one spade, although a doubleton is possible. His most likely shape is one spade, three hearts, five diamonds and four clubs. Should we bid four clubs? If partner is indeed 1-3-5-4, there would be 9+8 or 17 trumps. If we can make four clubs (ten tricks), we'd be better off collecting 300 against three spades doubled (seven tricks). We have our answer. Even if partner has a singleton spade there will be only 17 trumps (not to mention the potential minor honor problem — see Chapter Nine). There are not enough trumps to pull this double.

This same auction appears in the ACBL's write-up of the 1986 World Contract Bridge Championships in Miami.

Roman Smolski of Great Britain was a defender on this deal from the third session of the Open Pairs semifinal:

Neither Vul.
Dealer West

```
                    ♠ 2
                    ♡ K 10 7
                    ◇ A K Q J 7
                    ♣ 10 9 5 3
   ♠ A J 8 3                        ♠ K Q 9 7 5
   ♡ Q 9 5          N               ♡ 8 6 2
   ◇ 9 8 6 2     W     E            ◇ 5 3
   ♣ 6 4            S               ♣ K 7 2
                    ♠ 10 6 4
                    ♡ A J 4 3
                    ◇ 10 4
                    ♣ A Q J 8
```

West	North	East	South
Smolski	D. Siebert	Bethe	A. Siebert
pass	1◇	1♠	dbl
3♠	dbl	pass	4♡
all pass			

After David Siebert (USA) opened one diamond and Henry Bethe overcalled one spade, Allan Siebert made a negative double. Smolski raised preemptively to three spades, and David doubled to show a full opening bid and a willingness to compete further. Allan tried four hearts which closed the auction. Roman attacked with the six of clubs, which went to the three, king and ace. Now declarer played a heart to the king and passed the heart ten which won!

On the third heart Allan, figuring the hands were unbalanced because of the fast auction, played the jack. The Britons cashed three spade tricks for down one and 161 out of 166 matchpoints...

Nice defense, but what the write-up failed to mention was the merit of Siebert's four-heart bid — or lack of it. South should expect that there are nine spades and seven hearts, for a total of 16 trumps. He should know from the Law of Total Tricks that he should defend. If he had followed the LAW, he'd have been +500 against three spades doubled, and Smolski would have been deprived of his opportunity to shine.

In the semifinals of the 1986 Olympiad in Miami, Nisar Ahmed of Pakistan judged very well when he sat East and held the following hand with nobody vulnerable:

♠ J 7 4 ♡ 8 7 4 ◊ 10 8 6 4 ♣ 7 6 3

His partner opened with a strong and artificial two clubs, and Ron Rubin, of the United States, jumped preemptively to three spades. Nisar passed this around to his partner, who doubled. Nisar followed the theme prevalent in this chapter and passed the double. This was the full deal:

Neither Vul.
Dealer South

	♠ K 10 9 8 6 5 3	
	♡ 6	
	◊ 9	
	♣ Q 8 5 2	
♠ A 2	N	♠ J 7 4
♡ A K Q	W E	♡ 8 7 4
◊ A Q 5 3	S	◊ 10 8 6 4
♣ K J 10 9		♣ 7 6 3
	♠ Q	
	♡ J 10 9 5 3 2	
	◊ K J 7 2	
	♣ A 4	

Rubin lost two tricks in each black suit, and one in each red suit for -300. In the other room, Zia opened the South hand with a weak two-heart bid, and Weichsel-Lawrence (East-West) ended up in three notrump, down three, for a 10-IMP swing to the Pakistanis. Pakistan won the match by 5 IMPs, and went on to the finals to play for the World Championship.

Try this hand. Both vulnerable at IMPs, you're dealt

♠ K Q 10 9   ♡ 10 7 5 2   ◇ A Q 10 8 4   ♣ —

Your partner opens the bidding with one club and you soon find yourself confronted with the following decision:

Partner	RHO	You	LHO
1♣	1♡	dbl	2♡
2♠	3◇	dbl	3♡
pass	pass	??	

You chose to make a negative double and were pleased to hear your partner bid two spades. As you were about to raise to four spades, your RHO surprised you with a bid of three diamonds. You decided to double, and not surprisingly, LHO took out to three hearts which was passed back to you. You are about to go ahead and bid four spades, but how about a quick check on the LAW? It seems pretty clear that both sides have eight trumps for a total of 16. Why should we try for +620 (ten tricks), when we rate to have +800 (six tricks) against three hearts doubled? Besides, who says we're guaranteed to make four spades? The hand is unquestionably a misfit, and our diamond holding suggests that the opponents aren't going to have very many tricks after repeated trump leads! Come to think of it, double is a standout — and this was the full deal:

Both Vul.
Dealer North

```
                    ♠ A J 5 3
                    ♡ 8
                    ◇ 9 5
                    ♣ A Q 10 8 7 2
    ♠ 7 6 4 2              N           ♠ 8
    ♡ Q J 6          W         E       ♡ A K 9 4 3
    ◇ 3                    S           ◇ K J 7 6 2
    ♣ K J 9 6 3                        ♣ 5 4
                    ♠ K Q 10 9
                    ♡ 10 7 5 2
                    ◇ A Q 10 8 4
                    ♣ —
```

Can North-South make four spades? It's hard to say. But it's easy to see what happens to three hearts doubled on a trump lead. The best declarer can do is take five heart tricks in his hand and one diamond ruff in dummy for a penalty of 800. When this deal arose in actual play, South jumped to four spades, and after a heart lead, a trump shift, and a long struggle, North was defeated one trick.

On the last deal of the finals of the 1976 Bermuda Bowl in Monte Carlo, Arturo Franco had a chance to gain a sizable swing for Italy against the USA. He was holding

♠ 10 9 7 2   ♡ 10 9 8 5   ◇ J 10 8   ♣ J 4

vulnerable against not. This was the decision he faced:

West	North	East	South
Franco	Hamilton	Garozzo	Eisenberg
pass	1♣	dbl	3♡
pass	pass	dbl	pass
??			

What would you do? Use the LAW, of course. We expect partner to have at least two hearts (given his original takeout double), so the opponents have at most seven trumps. We certainly don't have too many trumps our way, at most an eight-card fit. So, there are at most 15 trumps and 15 tricks. If three hearts doubled were to make (-530), we'd probably be -300 if we played the hand. More likely, neither side can make their contract at this relatively high level. There are only going to be 14 or 15 tricks! Pass is clearly indicated, and was the winning action. Partner's hand was

♠ A J 6 3   ♡ A 4   ◇ A K 4 2   ♣ K 5 3

Franco chose to bid three spades, and missed his chance.

The same sort of decision was faced by one of America's best, Robert Levin, in the finals of the 1991 Spingold, played in Las Vegas. In the fourth quarter (on Vugraph) he held

♠ J 8 2   ♡ 8 4 2   ◇ 8 6 5   ♣ K J 6 4

vulnerable against not, as dealer. He passed and Jeff Meckstroth on his left opened a weak notrump (10-12). His partner, Peter Weichsel, doubled and Eric Rodwell on his right bid two natural diamonds. Levin passed, and Meckstroth raised preemptively to three diamonds, which Weichsel doubled:

Levin	Meckstroth	Weichsel	Rodwell
pass	1NT[1]	dbl	2◊[2]
pass	3◊	dbl	pass
??			

1.   10-12.
2.   Natural.

Levin could have passed and collected +300 to win 9 IMPs, but he cautiously pulled to four clubs, down 200, and lost 3 IMPs. Levin made the call that most experts would have. It's considered 'disciplined' to remove doubles in this situation, to avoid bringing back a score of -470 to your teammates. Eventually the expert community will begin to realize that they keep losing 5-10 IMPs by bidding in this situation, and they'll be willing to invest an occasional 10 IMPS (for -470) to put a stop to all the small 'disciplined' losses. In other words, they will start to obey the LAW.

Throughout this section we have repeatedly seen that we should be tempted to defend a doubled three-level contract. On many of these occasions, we have known, or suspected, that the opponents have a nine-card fit. So, in effect, we are going against the LAW, in that the opponents should be 'happy' to be at the three-level with nine trumps. What is the reason for this 'contradiction'?

In general, the opponents are indeed 'happy' to be at the three-level with their nine trumps. On many hands, our side could have made our two- or three-level contract, and now the opponents are simply offering us the opportunity to defeat them one trick (for +50, +100, or +200 depending upon the vulnerability, and whether or not we double) instead of handing us a score of +110 or +140. Also, they hope we will push on to the four-level and be defeated.

Sometimes, we just have to allow them to play at the three-level with nine trumps. The alternative of bidding one more would violate the LAW from our side's perspective. If they have nine trumps, and we have only seven or eight, there is not much we can do. The least of evils will be to defend their contract and hope that both sides have only eight tricks. Going on over their three-level contract without enough trumps is worse than allowing them to play at the three-level with their nine trumps.

Many times, throughout this section, we have doubled the opponents at the three-level to show 'cards'. Passing might feel dangerous but, in most cases, we will defeat them in spite of their nine trumps, because our overall high-card strength will usually see to it that they can't take as many as nine tricks.

Good news for anyone who is having trouble stomaching the thought of all these hair-raising leave-ins of three-level doubles: we're about to revisit the two-level, where the Law of Total Tricks usually argues in favor of pulling any doubles.

DECISIONS AT THE TWO-LEVEL

Most of the early portion of this book has been devoted to a discussion of the futility of letting the opponents play at the two-level when they have a fit. Whether doubled or not, the opponents will be quite happy at the two-level if they have eight trumps.

When the opponents open with a weak two-bid and partner makes a takeout double, we are not going to be very anxious to leave it in. No, they didn't bid and raise the suit, but lots of times opener will have six and responder two, and they will have an eight-card fit. If we're in doubt as to whether or not to leave the double in, position will have a lot to do with it. If we're behind (or over) the preemptor with a reasonable four-card trump holding, we might be tempted to leave in the double. However, if we have fewer than four trumps, we won't even consider passing a takeout double of a weak two-bid.

Following are some decisions on whether or not to defend after partner has doubled the opponents' weak two-bid. On all of these hands we are playing matchpoints, not vulnerable against vulnerable opponents. They have dealt and opened two spades, which we passed around to our partner, who doubled:

We	LHO	Partner	RHO
			2♠
pass	pass	dbl	pass
??			

♠ Q 10 5 2   ♡ A 8 7   ◇ Q 3 2   ♣ J 3 2

The only option, other than pass, would be to bid two notrump, which many people use as conventional. To bid three-of-a-suit would really go against the LAW. Pass rates to be a long-run winning action.

♠ K 10 8 4 ♡ 3 2 ◊ Q 6 4 2 ♣ J 4 3

Pass is a good gamble at matchpoints. Opposite 1-4-4-4 there will be 16 Total Trumps, but our ten of spades argues for a reduction in the expected number of tricks (see Chapter Nine).

♠ A 6 4 3 ♡ Q 4 3 2 ◊ 6 5 ♣ J 3 2

Here, pass is a possibility, but it is just too likely that they can make it. Our spade spots are not good enough.

Other doubles at the two-level aren't going to be left in very often. When we looked at auctions where the opponents jump raised to the three-level, we often left the double in. They had eight or nine trumps and we didn't have enough trumps to go to the four-level. However, on lower levels, there will be enough Total Trumps to justify competing in our side's long suit. It's hard to get rich defending two-level contracts when the opponents have eight trumps. There's got to be a very good reason to do so!

One further word about doubles on all-levels. Be extremely wary of voids in the opponents' suit, as illustrated by this hand from the Australia-Sweden match in the 1977 Bermuda Bowl played in Manila:

Both Vul.
Dealer East

```
                        ♠ A K 3
                        ♡ 10 9 4
                        ◊ 9 5 4 3
                        ♣ K 8 3
  ♠ Q 10 9 8 7 5 4   ┌─────────────┐   ♠ J 6 2
  ♡ 5 3              │      N      │   ♡ K 8 7 6
  ◊ 10               │ W         E │   ◊ A J 8 7
  ♣ 9 7 6            │      S      │   ♣ A 4
                     └─────────────┘
                        ♠ —
                        ♡ A Q J 2
                        ◊ K Q 6 2
                        ♣ Q J 10 5 2
```

West	North	East	South
Borin	Brunzell	Havas	Lindquist
		1NT (12-14)	dbl
2♠	dbl	all pass	

The Swedish South player was guilty of an all-too-common error in competitive bidding. He doubled his opponents' weak notrump, heard his partner double the runout to two spades — and left it in with a void! Most good partnerships play North's double as 'card-showing'. It tends to show at least two cards (usually three or more) in the suit bid, and enough points to warrant getting into the auction.

Here's why we have a problem with South's sitting for the double. Even over penalty doubles, we try very hard never to defend with a void in trumps. For one thing, it makes the hand extremely hard to defend because we can never get in to lead a trump through — which is often what partner wants when defending low-level contracts. Secondly (and most importantly), our void suggests that the opponents have a lot of trumps — probably enough to be LAW-satisfied. Especially at low-levels, the opponents almost surely have as many trumps as the level to which they have bid.

A frequent error is to look at your void, hear partner double, and say, 'Partner must have quite a trump stack — let's defend.' This is not good thinking. On the deal above, where the opponents are at the two-level, they rate to have at least eight, and often nine trumps. (On the actual deal it was ten — and North-South missed an easy vulnerable game. They also misdefended and let two spades doubled make!)

When using the LAW, both partners must be wary of doubling (or leaving doubles in) with voids. Partner, in making Law of Total Tricks decisions, will usually not play you for a void. When he assumes shortness in your hand, he expects a singleton. And, as we noted before, it's hard to defend with a void since you can never lead trumps. When we open the bidding (say, with one spade), and their overcall (say, two clubs) is passed back around to us, we are very reluctant to reopen double with a void. Yes, we know partner is usually hoping we will double (so he can convert for penalties), but our void often makes defending too difficult. Declarer usually scrambles too many tricks because we can't lead trumps. Here is a typical example:

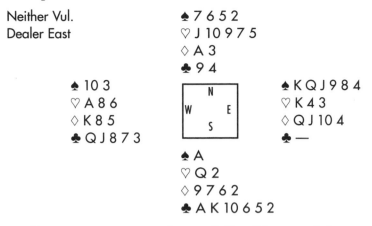

Neither Vul.
Dealer East

```
                      ♠ 7 6 5 2
                      ♡ J 10 9 7 5
                      ◇ A 3
                      ♣ 9 4
    ♠ 10 3                              ♠ K Q J 9 8 4
    ♡ A 8 6          ┌─────────┐       ♡ K 4 3
    ◇ K 8 5          │    N    │       ◇ Q J 10 4
    ♣ Q J 8 7 3      │ W     E │       ♣ —
                     │    S    │
                     └─────────┘
                      ♠ A
                      ♡ Q 2
                      ◇ 9 7 6 2
                      ♣ A K 10 6 5 2
```

East opens one spade, and South's two-club overcall is passed around to him. In the old days, the auction would have gone **1♠ —2♣ —Penalty Double**. In either case, East should be wary of defending with a void. He should bid two spades and not get involved with doubling. The potential dummy for two clubs doubled isn't surprising. When we have a trump void, we can usually expect dummy to have a little bit of support.

Similarly when the auction goes something like **1♡ —pass —2♡** to us, we're also reluctant to double with a void. Too often, partner will leave it in (with say, Q10xxx of hearts), and we won't be able to beat them. We also try to avoid doubling four-level openings with voids. Over a four-spade opening bid we'd prefer four notrump (takeout) versus a double, with shapes such as 0-4-5-4 or 0-5-3-5, or 0-3-5-5, etc. Too often, partner will pass the double, and we'll be defending a ten-card fit!

CHAPTER REVIEW

- There is a tendency for players to allow themselves to be pushed up in the bidding. If we know that there aren't enough Total Trumps, we should try hard not to 'bid one more' over the opponents' high-level preempts.

- It's important for the partnership to have a firm understanding of what a double of the opponents' four-of-a-major opening bid shows.

- Before taking out a double of four-of-a-major, try to figure out how many trumps there rate to be. There will usually not be enough to warrant bidding. Use the 'chart' concept to see what the score would be if you were to play the hand as opposed to defending.

- Leaving in three-level doubles (especially when the opponents have nine trumps) feels very risky, but is often the winning action. You must be prepared for an occasional -530 in exchange for a lot of +100's and +300's. You can't afford to keep being pushed to the four-level, when neither side can take more than eight tricks!

- When the opponents are at the two-level with eight trumps, it's a different story. The two-level is low enough that there will almost always be enough trumps to warrant competing in our own suit.

- Be reluctant to defend when you have a void in the opponents' trump suit.

1) Your partner doubles the opponent's four-heart opening. Your agreement is that this is takeout.

   a) What number of hearts will we assume that partner holds on average?

   b) How many spades should we play him for?

2) Your hand is

   ♠ K 5 3 2 ♡ K 4 2 ◇ A 10 5 ♣ 10 8 7

   Your partner makes a takeout double of their four-heart opening with nobody vulnerable in a Swiss Team match. Use your answers from Question 1 and answer the following:

   a) How many hearts should we assume the opponents have?

   b) How many trumps (spades) should we assume we have?

   c) How many Total Trumps (Tricks) should there be?

   d) Is there any reasonable way those tricks can be split whereby bidding four spades will produce a better score than defending four hearts doubled?

   e) If you used adjustments as discussed in Chapter Three, what might this cause you to do to your answer to (c)?

   f) What does the LAW say to do?

3) Your hand is

   ♠ A J 10 3 ♡ A 5 ◇ K J 9 3 ♣ 8 7 6

   and vulnerable against not you hear this auction:

You	LHO	Partner	RHO
1◇	1♡	dbl	3♡
pass	pass	dbl	pass
??			

Partner's first double was negative ('promising' four spades). His double of their preemptive raise showed 'cards' and at least two cards in their suit. What does the LAW tell us to do, and why?

4) Your hand is

♠ A J 10   ♡ A 5   ♢ K J 9 2   ♣ 8 7 6 2

with the same conditions and same auction as above. What does the LAW say now?

5) Both sides are vulnerable at matchpoints and you hold

♠ K Q 6   ♡ 7 4 2   ♢ A 9 7   ♣ 10 6 4 3

Your LHO opens three hearts, partner doubles, and it's up to you.

CHAPTER 6 ANSWERS

1) **a)** One
   b) Four

2) **a)** Nine
   b) Eight
   c) 17
   d) No! Our score defending four hearts doubled will always be better than playing in four spades (unless they make it, but that is extremely unlikely).
   e) Subtract — use 16½ or 16. Your king of hearts is a very big negative adjustment factor — especially if you are behind the four-heart bidder! More on this in Chapter Nine.
   f) Pass!

3) Bid three spades. We assume 17 trumps (eight for us and nine for them), and think in 'chart' terms as follows. 'If we can beat three hearts doubled (+100), then we can take

nine tricks ourselves (+140). If they are making three hearts doubled, then we'd better bid three spades and go down one. If the tricks are split ten for us and seven for them, pass would work out (unless partner plans to raise to game!).'

4) Pass. They probably have nine trumps, but this time our eight-card fit (in one of the minors) would take us to the four-level. We don't want to be there with only 17 trumps. The most likely scenario is that they have eight tricks in hearts and we have nine tricks in our minor. They might make three hearts doubled one time in ten. Bidding will turn a plus into a minus almost all of the time. It's worth incurring one -530 rather than turning nine +100's into nine -100's.

5) This hand was presented in *The Bridge World*, December 1991, Master Solvers column. Pass was the top vote-getter from the expert panel, including this comment from David Berah: 'Pass... As a Law-of-Total-Tricks disciple, I have learned to do these routinely at matchpoints. I expect a plus score, which I am very uncertain of if I bid.'

NOTRUMP AND THE LAW

CHAPTER 7

Decisions as to whether or not to compete against the opponents' notrump contract are not as common as those against a suit contract. Sacrifices against three notrump are rare, and competing against an opposition two-notrump contract is even more uncommon. We've already touched upon the advantages of balancing against one notrump in our discussion of D.O.N.T. in Chapter Four. Is there a formula for Total Tricks when one side is playing in notrump? In Vernes' *Bridge Moderne de la Defense* * he presented a somewhat confusing chart dealing with this subject. My own way of dealing with notrump and the LAW is a bit different.

On a normal deal, if both sides played in notrump contracts, you would expect 13 Total Tricks. If one side can make nine tricks without a trump suit, it follows that the other side can make only four. Of course, the fact that one side has the opening lead is relevant, but, as a generalization, 13 Total Tricks will be the expectancy.

If we add a trump suit the picture changes. We saw in Chapter One that, if each side has seven trumps, we expect 14 Total Tricks. If each side has eight trumps, then we expect 16 Total Tricks. What if only one side has a trump suit?

The side playing in notrump will still have the same number of tricks: if the notrumpers had nine in notrump, and the other side had four in notrump, the notrumpers will still have nine, even when the other side is contemplating playing in a suit contract. The opponents, with the aid of a trump suit will, of course, have more than four tricks.

How many more? That depends upon how many trumps they have. For each trump starting with seven, they will have one additional trick. If they have seven trumps, and the opponents have nine tricks at notrump, they will still have their original four (notrump) tricks, plus an additional one (for the seventh trump), making five tricks, and 14 Total Tricks for the deal. If they have eight trumps (and the opponents still have nine tricks) they would have six tricks (the four they could take in notrump, plus two for the extra trumps). With nine trumps, they'd have seven tricks, and so on...

---

* In 1966 Jean-René Vernes first wrote about the Law of Total Tricks .

This leads us to state a simple formula:

> The number of Total Tricks, when side A plays in
> notrump and side B plays in a trump suit = seven
> plus the number of trumps held by side B

So, if your side has eight trumps, and the opponents are in notrump, then there are 7+8, or 15 Total Tricks. If you have nine trumps, then there are 7+9, or 16 Total Tricks.

How do we apply this to our competitive decisions? If your opponents are in three notrump, and you expect them to make exactly nine tricks, what are your prospects of sacrificing successfully? If your side has ten trumps, you can expect to take your four tricks (at notrump) plus four more tricks (for the seventh, eighth, ninth, and tenth trumps). Or, using the formula, you can expect 7+10, or 17 Total Tricks. So, if they're making three notrump (nine tricks), then your sacrifice would yield 17-9, or eight tricks.

This formula assumes relatively normal distribution. There are two obvious factors which will affect the Total Trick count at notrump. The first factor is the notrumpers' possession of a long suit to run. If they are playing in notrump after one of them has implied a long suit (six cards or longer), there will tend to be extra tricks. For each card in their long suit starting with the sixth, there will be one additional trick. A typical auction that shows a long suit is one where they open one-of-a-minor and jump rebid three notrump. Another example is when they open with a preempt and then get to three notrump.

The second factor is good side-suit distribution for your side. If you have a singleton, there will usually be one-half to one extra trick. If your side has a void, there will usually be a full extra trick. Of course, this is not an exact science. However, awareness of the basic formula, along with these two subtle adjustment factors, can be very useful.

Notice how this formula fits in with D.O.N.T., which helped us to compete against one notrump. We saw in Chapter Four how hard we want to try to find an eight-card fit at the two-level when the opponents open one notrump. You can now see that if we have an eight-card fit against their one notrump contract there will be 15 Total Tricks. So, if they are making one notrump, we can expect to make our two-level contract! And, if they're making two (+120), then we're only going down one at the two-level.

Knowing that the LAW supports interfering against one notrump is the most useful application for the 'Notrump Formula'. Let's look at some 'Notrump and the LAW' decisions from actual play.

In the 1978 World Pairs Championships in New Orleans, Marcello Branco, on his way to victory, picked up:

♠ A K 5 4   ♡ Q 8 7 6 3 2   ◇ —   ♣ K Q 2

With nobody vulnerable his RHO opened an 11-14 notrump, Branco bid two clubs to show the majors, and the auction proceeded:

RHO	Branco	LHO	Cintra
1NT[1]	2♣[2]	2♡[3]	3♡
3NT	??		

1. 11-14.
2. Majors.
3. Minors.

Instinct told Branco to bid four hearts, where he was doubled and scored +590. What would the LAW have told him to do? His partner bid three hearts without many points, so there was an excellent chance of his having four-card support. That gives his side 10 trumps, which added to 7 (from the formula) makes 17. The opponents could easily have a running six-card diamond suit, so the total could even be 18. Certainly, there are enough tricks to warrant bidding four hearts over three notrump, since both sides rate to have about nine tricks.

This last hand had unusual distribution, making it worthwhile to compete over the opponents' three-notrump contract. On the vast majority of hands, not enough shape will be present, and the LAW will suggest defending. In the 1979 Bermuda Bowl in Rio de Janeiro, Italy faced America (as usual) in the final, and Italy's Vito Pittala could have benefited from this advice. He held a 4-3-3-3 six-count, and sacrificed over three notrump on the following auction:

West	North	East	South
Kantar	Belladonna	Eisenberg	Pittala
	pass	1♣	pass
3♣	3♢	pass	pass
3NT	pass	pass	??

He was at favorable vulnerability, but the notrump formula would have told him to pass. He'd figure on eight or nine trumps for his side (probably only eight from his partner's failure to preempt originally), for a likely total of only 15. His opponents might have had six running clubs to get the count up to 16 tricks, but still, sacrificing would only be right if the tricks were split exactly seven for him and nine for the opponents (-500 instead of -600). This was the full deal:

E-W Vul.
North Dealer

```
                  ♠ A 9
                  ♡ J 8 7 4
                  ◇ K Q 6 5 4
                  ♣ 9 2
    ♠ 6 4 3              N           ♠ J 10 7 2
    ♡ A 10 5         W       E       ♡ K Q 6
    ◇ A 10               S           ◇ J 8 2
    ♣ Q 10 7 6 5                     ♣ A K 8
                  ♠ K Q 8 5
                  ♡ 9 3 2
                  ◇ 9 7 3
                  ♣ J 4 3
```

The Californians doubled four diamonds and defended well (cashing three hearts and two clubs and eventually scoring the trump jack via an uppercut on the fourth round of clubs), for a four-trick defeat. Fortunately for Pittala, three notrump happened to be cold, so his loss was minimal.

In the 1975 World Championships in Bermuda, the two legendary pairs of the seventies opposed each other. Giorgio Belladonna, of Italy, held:

♠ Q J 7 3   ♡ J   ◇ Q 6 5 3   ♣ K Q J 8

and opened the bidding one diamond. Bobby Wolff, of the United States, overcalled one spade, and Benito Garozzo made a negative double. The auction continued as follows (the Americans were vulnerable against not):

Belladonna	Wolff	Garozzo	Hamman
1◇	1♠	dbl	pass
1NT	2♠	pass	pass
??			

Belladonna bid two notrump which bought the contract. He was down one for -50, instead of getting the plus score he could have registered against two spades. As Henry Francis wrote, 'Belladonna could have gained a few IMPs had he curbed his competitive inclinations and allowed Wolff to play in two spades.'

In other words, if Belladonna had used the LAW he would have passed. The opponents rated to have only seven spades, since Garozzo would probably have competed if he had a singleton. The notrump formula would indicate 7+7, or 14 Total Tricks, making it futile to compete to two notrump (both sides rate to be down one).

A very similar 'error in judgment' was made by the fine American player, Eddie Wold. Playing in the 1986 World Pairs Championships in Miami, he was at unfavorable vulnerability, holding:

♠ A 8 5 2 ♡ 6 ◇ J 6 5 3 ♣ 6 5 3 2

Facing a French pair, he heard the following:

Covo	Compton	Paladino	Wold
pass	1♡	dbl	pass
1♠	3♡	pass	pass
3♠	pass	pass	??

Wold, as many experts might be tempted to do, bid three notrump. This was due to fail by at least two tricks, but partner took out to four hearts which was doubled, down one, -200. Quoting Phillip Alder in *The 1986 World Contract Bridge Championships*: '...3NT was brave but unlucky since three spades will fail...'

But are we surprised that both three spades and three notrump will fail? East-West could be expected to have seven or eight spades for a total of 14 or 15 tricks. They actually had only a 4-3 fit, since Compton's hand was

♠ 7 3 ♡ A J 10 8 7 5 4 2 ◇ K ♣ A 4

If Wold were able to make nine tricks in three notrump, then the opponents would have only five or six tricks in three spades doubled. More likely was what actually occurred — those 14 or 15 tricks were split seven or eight for each side.

It isn't quite fair to criticize Wold; if the hearts were running (say partner had AKQxxxx), then three notrump could be the big winner. In fact, the notrump formula suggests adding tricks for a long suit -- but, as this deal illustrates, unless the suit is running, there won't be any extra tricks! It's sometimes hard to tell during the bidding if the long suit will run. (Holdings such as honor-and-one in partner's long suit are obviously more of an indication that the suit will run than a small singleton would be.)

Auctions involving the LAW and notrump don't come up very frequently, but it's still worthwhile to keep the formula in mind. Kerri Shuman is widely regarded as the best female bridge player in the world, so I don't think she'll mind if I bring up one of her few bad hands. In 1990 she won the World Women's Pairs Championship in Geneva with Karen McCallum, despite this notrump LAW violation. She responded one heart to Karen's one-club opening, and soon faced this decision:

♠ A K Q   ♡ J 10 9 8 6   ◇ J 8 7 6   ♣ A

McCallum	Yia Lan	Shuman	Ling
1♣	pass	1♡	pass
3◇[1]	pass	3♠[2]	pass
4♡[3]	pass	4NT[4]	pass
5♣[5]	pass	5◇[6]	pass
5♡[7]	pass	6♡	pass
pass	6♠	??	

1. Forcing heart raise.
2. Asking.
3. Singleton spade.
4. Roman Key Card Blackwood.
5. 0 or 3 Key Cards.
6. Queen ask.
7. No queen.

Kerri bid six notrump in an attempt to score 1440 instead of taking the penalty against six spades doubled. She went down one in six notrump when six spades doubled would have been down seven or eight for +1700 or +2000! What does the LAW say? Her partner showed a singleton spade during the auction. Kerri knew the opponents had nine spades, and the formula says there would have been 7+9, or 16 Total Tricks. If you go through the possibilities you'll see that bidding six notrump could not have been the winning action.

CHAPTER REVIEW

- When deciding to compete against (or in) notrump, the LAW can still be applied.

- The Total Number of Tricks, when one side is in notrump and the other side is in a suit, is seven plus the number of trumps.

- Adjustments need to be made for long running suits, and for singletons and voids.

- The extremely beneficial advantages of D.O.N.T. (Chapter Four) are verified by the notrump formula.

- Decisions using the LAW in conjunction with notrump occur fairly infrequently. The conclusion will usually be that there are not enough Total Tricks to compete.

CHAPTER 7 QUESTIONS

1) You have ♠ A J 4 3 2 opposite ♠ 7 6 5 and there are no singletons or voids and no long suits. The opponents have reached three notrump with their 24 high-card points. How many Total Tricks are there likely to be?

2) When competing against one notrump, if you land at the two-level with an eight-card fit, what does the LAW suggest?

3) You have

   ♠ A J 7 6 5   ♡ J 10 6 4 2   ◊ 5 3 2   ♣ —

   and, with nobody vulnerable, the opponents opened one notrump. You overcalled two hearts to show majors, and their responder jumped to three notrump.

   a) Partner is looking at

      ♠ 8 3   ♡ Q 7 5   ◊ A 8 6 4   ♣ J 7 6 2

      How many Total Tricks might he expect if he assumes that you are 5-5 in the majors?

   b) Should that induce him to sacrifice in four hearts?

4) With both sides vulnerable, the opponents opened three diamonds, partner overcalled three hearts, and they bid three notrump. You are holding

   ♠ A 5 2   ♡ J 6 5   ◊ 4 3   ♣ Q J 10 6 2

   a) How many Total Tricks might you expect?

   b) Should you pass or bid four hearts?

5) You're in fourth seat at favorable vulnerability holding

   ♠ Q J 3   ♡ A K 9 8   ◊ J 6 4   ♣ 8 5 3

   Your partner doubles their three-heart opening. What should you do, and why?

CHAPTER 7 ANSWERS

1) 7+8, or 15 Total Tricks.

2) You are in excellent shape since there should be 15 Total Tricks. Both your contract and one notrump could be makable.

3) **a)** He should expect at least 7+8, or 15 Total Tricks. He could also add a half-trick if you have a singleton, or one if you have a void. So, he can count 15½ or 16 tricks.

b) No. He should not bid four hearts. Even if there are 16 tricks, the sacrifice will be more expensive than the value of three notrump (-500 vs. -400). On the two hands given, the defense should get at least two spades, two hearts and two diamonds if they prevent spade ruffs.

4) **a)** 7+9+1 = 17. Partner probably has six hearts, so we have nine trumps. Add at least one for their long diamond suit.

b) Bid four hearts. If there are 17 trumps, this will work out poorly only if they have eight tricks and we have nine. In any other case, one side or the other will be making game. Furthermore, if they have a running seven-card diamond suit, we can figure on 7+9+2 or 18 Total Tricks. In that case bidding four hearts must be right. Try the numbers!

5) Pass. To use the LAW, picture partner with a typical 4-1-4-4 shape. That means they have eight hearts, and using the notrump LAW formula we assume 7+8, or 15 tricks. If we can make nine tricks in three notrump (+400), they'd have only six tricks in three hearts doubled (+800).

LAW MAXIMS

CHAPTER 8

'Cover an honor with an honor.' 'Eight ever, nine never.' 'Fourth from your longest and strongest.'...

There are plenty of time-honored axioms relating to declarer play and defense. In this chapter, we will look at four *bidding* 'maxims' — all related to the Law of Total Tricks:

1) The five-level belongs to the opponents.

2) When in doubt, bid four spades over four hearts.

3) When in doubt, bid one more on freak deals.

4) When you hold four trumps, consider making a penalty double.

1) THE FIVE-LEVEL BELONGS TO THE OPPONENTS

We touched on this in Chapter Two, where we saw that competing at the five-level was not very productive. The logic is quite obvious. There have to be a lot of trumps for both sides to consider contracting for 11 tricks! No, there don't have to be 22 trumps, but it's an idea worth keeping in the back of your mind.

There are very few situations where the LAW dictates bidding five-over-five with fewer than 22 trumps. It's worthwhile to bid only if there is either (a) a good sacrifice, or (b) a higher score for making your contract than for defeating the opponents.

These two potentially profitable situations depend upon the vulnerability, but they still require a lot of trumps to be profitable. If we were to look at it in chart form, we'd see that, with fewer than 19 trumps, it will never be right to bid five-over-five. With 19 trumps, it will only be right when the tricks are split 11-8 and the vulnerability is right. Even when there are 20 trumps, bidding five-over-five will often be wrong — especially if each side has only ten tricks. How often will there be 21 or more trumps? Almost never! So then, **the five-level belongs to the opponents!**

Bidding five-over-five is an error that even the best players sometimes make. They fail to realize that to contract for 11 tricks yourself when the opponents have contracted for 11 requires an inordinate number of trumps. If you read a write-up of any long match, you will find frequent examples of players overbidding at the five-level. Think about the conditions which must be present for you to believe that there are 20 or more trumps!

In the finals of the Von Zedwitz, New York's year-long knockout event, Steve Sanborn, a member of the 1990 winning team, held:

♠ 7 4 3   ♡ 10 9 6 4 3   ◇ K 10 7 5 2   ♣ —

Fortunately, he's very aware of the LAW, and made the winning decision, vulnerable against not, after this auction:

West	North	East	South
	Rosner		Sanborn
3♣	dbl	5♣	pass
pass	dbl	pass	pass!
pass			

Steve's pass of the double would hardly be the choice of most experts, but it was winning action. This was the full deal :

N-S Vul.
Dealer West

```
                  ♠ A K Q 5
                  ♡ A J 7 2
                  ◇ Q J
                  ♣ 9 6 2
  ♠ J 10 2                        ♠ 9 8 6
  ♡ 5            ┌─────────┐      ♡ K Q 8
  ◇ 9 6 3        │    N    │      ◇ A 8 4
  ♣ K Q J 10 5 4 │ W     E │      ♣ A 8 7 3
                 │    S    │
                 └─────────┘
                  ♠ 7 4 3
                  ♡ 10 9 6 4 3
                  ◇ K 10 7 5 2
                  ♣ —
```

If Steve had bid five hearts, he would have been a little unfortunate to go down, but would still have been -100. The actual pass netted +500. The player at the other table faced the same auction and bid five diamonds, which was easily defeated. This illustrates one other problem with guessing to bid on at the five-level — you could easily wind up in the wrong suit. Even if you guess the right suit (hearts, in this case), there need to be at least 20 trumps for bidding to be profitable. Partner's double will often be based on a balanced strong notrump type of hand — he doesn't *guarantee* shortness in the opponents' suit.

On the following deal from the 1984 Seattle Olympiad, a good understanding of the Law of Total Tricks led to the winning decision by the North-South pair:

N-S Vul.
Dealer East

```
                    ♠ A K 9 2
                    ♡ J 9 6 5 3
                    ◇ J 10
                    ♣ J 9
    ♠ 7 6            ┌─────────┐        ♠ 10 4 3
    ♡ Q 4 2          │    N    │        ♡ 10 8 7
    ◇ K 9 8 5 2      │ W     E │        ◇ 4
    ♣ K 7 4          │    S    │        ♣ A Q 10 6 5 2
                    └─────────┘
                    ♠ Q J 8 5
                    ♡ A K
                    ◇ A Q 7 6 3
                    ♣ 8 3
```

West	North	East	South
Hamman	Burgess	Wolff	Marston
		3♣	dbl
5♣	pass	pass	dbl
all pass			

By partnership agreement, North's pass of five clubs was forcing, showing some values. South doubled again, and five clubs doubled was defeated four tricks.

The Australian North-South pair judged well to not get to the five-level, where they would have been defeated. The LAW makes this an easy decision. Marston and Burgess can each assume that their opponents have nine or ten clubs — for 9½. They, themselves, presumably have an eight or nine-card fit — for 8½. That makes a total of 18 trumps, which means that, if North-South can make 11 tricks, then East-West are taking only seven. That being the case, there is no need to bid game, since the score for defending five clubs doubled will be better. Obviously, as is the case here, if North-South have fewer than 11 tricks, it is even more clear to defend.

As we have seen, to bid on at such a high level normally requires at least 20 trumps — think about it in chart form as explained in Chapter Two. On the actual deal there were only 17 trumps, and 17 tricks.

Experts throughout the world can be found bidding too much at the five level — over and over again. Britain's star pair, Andy Robson and Tony Forrester, seemed to win every European event in the early 1990s, but it wasn't due to decisions like this next one. At favorable colors, Robson heard Forrester deal and open four spades in the finals of the 1991 Koning en Hartman Championship (IMP scoring). Robson's opponent overcalled five clubs and Andy was looking at

♠ 8 3   ♡ A 10 9 7 6 2   ◇ A 8 5 2   ♣ 4

It shouldn't take any charts to know that it's wrong to bid five spades (which is what Robson did). His partner was 7-1-3-2, and five spades had no legitimate play. Doubling five clubs would have yielded +800.

There are rare occasions where bidding five-over-five can be right. Consider this deal from the 1991 World Juniors Championship in Ann Arbor, Michigan:

Both Vul.
Dealer East

```
                    ♠ A 9 7 5 4 2
                    ♡ 6 4
                    ◇ A 9 2
                    ♣ 7 4
    ♠ 8                               ♠ 6
    ♡ K J 10 9 8 5 3    ┌─────────┐   ♡ A Q 7 2
    ◇ 5                 │    N    │   ◇ J 10 4 3
    ♣ Q 9 3 2           │ W     E │   ♣ A K J 6
                        │    S    │
                        └─────────┘
                    ♠ K Q J 10 3
                    ♡ —
                    ◇ K Q 8 7 6
                    ♣ 10 8 5
```

The American team defended five spades in one room and were -710 after a diamond lead. Their teammates, sitting North-South in the other room, sold out to five hearts and went -650 to lose 16 IMPs. If North-South had known there were 22 trumps, they surely would not have sold out to five hearts! Of course, this was an abnormal deal.

Our last five-level example reverts to form:

Both Vul.
Dealer South

```
                      ♠ 9 5 3
                      ♡ 10 9 8 3
                      ◇ —
                      ♣ J 9 7 6 3 2
    ♠ A K J                          ♠ Q 10 7 6 4
    ♡ Q 6 5          ┌─────────┐     ♡ 2
    ◇ A Q 9          │    N    │     ◇ J 8 5 4
    ♣ Q 10 5 4       │ W     E │     ♣ A K 8
                     │    S    │
                     └─────────┘
                      ♠ 8 2
                      ♡ A K J 7 4
                      ◇ K 10 7 6 3 2
                      ♣ —
```

West	North	East	South
			1♡
1NT	3♡[1]	4♠	5♡
pass	pass	5♠	pass
pass	dbl	all pass	

1. Weak.

On this deal from the 1991 European Championships, East-West outbid their opponents at the five-level when there were only 17 trumps. This, as you know by now, was not a good decision! The defense was merciless. After the king of hearts lead, five cross-ruffs followed for down four and -1100! Both West and East should have known to double five hearts — there weren't enough trumps to bid on.

2) WHEN IN DOUBT, BID FOUR SPADES OVER FOUR HEARTS

In the 1985 Bermuda Bowl in São Paulo, Chip Martel of the United States held

♠ K 9 7 4 3 2   ♡ 9   ◇ A 10 5 2   ♣ 10 9

with both sides vulnerable. He faced the following decision as West playing against Austria:

West	North	East	South
Martel	*Meinl*	*Stansby*	*Berger*
			pass
pass	1♡	pass	1NT
2♠	3♡	3♠	4♡
??			

He had only seven high-card points opposite a passed hand. The title of this section notwithstanding, could one of America's best players have actually bid four spades?

We saw in Chapter Six that we should usually leave in partner's double of a four-of-a-major opening bid. This was especially true if they opened four spades, and we had to go to the five-level to take out the double. It doesn't often happen that there are enough trumps to warrant competing to the five-level — just look at the examples in the last section! However, competing at the four-level has a higher frequency of being correct. The most profitable four-over-four action is competing to four spades when the opponents have bid to four hearts.

To bid four spades over four hearts is a decision that should absolutely be based on the LAW. It still pays to go through the 'chart' in your mind, considering what would happen if each side were to take such-and-such a number of tricks. Primarily because both contracts carry a game bonus, you'll find that it's often profitable to bid four spades over four hearts.

For example, with neither vulnerable, let's assume that there are 18 trumps; the opponents have bid to four hearts, and we are contemplating competing to four spades. In chart form, here are the three most likely scenarios:

CHART FOR 18 TOTAL TRICKS
Nobody Vulnerable

We play the hand in four spades		They play the hand in four hearts	
Our Tricks	Our Score	Their Tricks	Our Score
10	**+420**	8	+100/300
9	−50/100	9	**+50/100**
8	**−100/300**	10	−420

Notice that the chart shows scores for eight and nine tricks as either undoubled or doubled. Especially take note of the fact that only in the 'nine-and-nine' scenario is competing to four spades the losing action — and then only by a small margin! If you compare this chart (and try all possible vulnerabilities) to some of the other charts, you'll see that bidding four spades over four hearts doesn't require as many trumps as you would expect.

Again, don't get too involved with the charts (or trying to memorize them). Every competitive problem can be solved via the simple process of counting the trumps and going through the math in your head. The point here is that, as a shortcut, it's a reasonable general rule to say, 'When in doubt, bid four spades over four hearts'.

Let's return to Chip Martel's decision in Brazil. He held

♠ K 9 7 4 3 2   ♡ 9   ◇ A 10 5 2   ♣ 10 9

with both sides vulnerable, and faced the following problem:

West	North	East	South
Martel	*Meinl*	*Stansby*	*Berger*
			pass
pass	1♡	pass	1NT
2♠	3♡	3♠	4♡
??			

It seems quite bold, but he bid four spades. Clearly, his experience taught him that bidding four spades over four hearts in this kind of auction is a winning proposition.

This was the full deal:

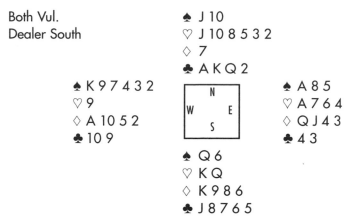

Both Vul.
Dealer South

```
                    ♠ J 10
                    ♡ J 10 8 5 3 2
                    ◇ 7
                    ♣ A K Q 2
♠ K 9 7 4 3 2                           ♠ A 8 5
♡ 9                 ┌─────────┐        ♡ A 7 6 4
◇ A 10 5 2          │    N    │        ◇ Q J 4 3
♣ 10 9             W│         │E        ♣ 4 3
                    │    S    │
                    └─────────┘
                    ♠ Q 6
                    ♡ K Q
                    ◇ K 9 8 6
                    ♣ J 8 7 6 5
```

Martel was doubled in four spades, and ended up +990 when the defense slipped and allowed an overtrick. In some respects, Martel was fortunate to find a double fit. It's important to note that the IMP scale makes bidding four spades a big winner when you find a double fit, but only a small-to-medium loser when both four spades and four hearts are down a trick. If one contract makes and the other fails by a trick, bidding four spades is always the winning action. After reading Chapter Nine it will be easier to understand why there are so many Total Tricks on this deal.

The following decision comes from the 1978 Rosenblum Teams in New Orleans. When the U.S.A. opposed New Zealand, the South players held the following cards:

♠ K Q 10 8 5 4 ♡ 9 ◇ K 6 5 ♣ J 8 7

Vulnerable against non-vulnerable opponents they heard: **4♡ — pass — pass**.

Bidding at this vulnerability seems dangerous, and most players wouldn't dream of it. Even believers in our 'maxim' ('when in *doubt...*') would pass — they wouldn't be in *doubt!*

However, let's do a little thinking along the lines of the LAW. The four-heart bidder will often have an eight-card suit. We have one heart and, on balance, partner and RHO will each have two. So, let's say that the opponents rate to have ten hearts. Also LHO, who has eight cards in hearts, figures to have a lot of short side-suits — especially spades, where his probable holding is a singleton. The other spades rate to be split three for partner and three for RHO. That would mean that our side has nine spades.

Granted, none of these estimates have to be right, but bridge is a game of percentages. If you always assign distributions within expected percentages, you will, in the long run, be correct often enough to show a big profit. In any event, going with percentages is better than guessing.

Ten hearts for them plus nine spades for us means that there are 19 trumps, and 19 tricks. That tells us to bid four spades. If the tricks are split ten and nine this will show a huge profit. Even if they are split 11 and eight, it will be only slightly wrong to go -500, as opposed to -450 defending four hearts.

The New Zealand player passed and went -420. Fred Hamilton of the United States made the bold four-spade bid and was justly rewarded:

```
N-S Vul.                    ♠ A 9 7
Dealer West                 ♡ 6
                            ◇ A J 10 9 7 3 2
                            ♣ Q 9
      ♠ 2                 ┌──────────┐      ♠ J 6 3
      ♡ A Q J 8 7 4 3 2   │    N     │      ♡ K 10 5
      ◇ 8                 │ W     E  │      ◇ Q 4
      ♣ 10 6 2            │    S     │      ♣ A K 5 4 3
                         └──────────┘
                            ♠ K Q 10 8 5 4
                            ♡ 9
                            ◇ K 6 5
                            ♣ J 8 7
```

East competed to five hearts and North bid on to five spades which was defeated by one trick, but this was still a much better score than the -420 recorded at the other table. Granted, South was lucky to find a total of 20 trumps, but certainly the 20 that existed were only one away from the 19 that would be expected over the long haul. Even if there turned out to be only 18 trumps, four spades wouldn't be a disaster. If there were only 16 or 17 trumps, and South went for 800, I hope it wouldn't deter him from making what is the long-run winning decision in the future.

Incidentally, when you know that your side has a good heart fit, and you bid up to four hearts, don't you just hate it when the opponents bid four spades? Some of bridge's most annoying 'guesses' occur when they save in four spades over four hearts, and you have to decide whether to double or go on to five hearts.

The following World Championship deal illustrates the importance of bidding quickly to four spades in competition:

Neither Vul.
Dealer West

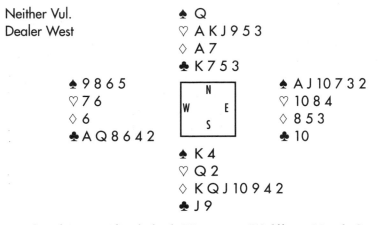

```
                      ♠ Q
                      ♡ A K J 9 5 3
                      ◇ A 7
                      ♣ K 7 5 3
  ♠ 9 8 6 5                             ♠ A J 10 7 3 2
  ♡ 7 6              N                   ♡ 10 8 4
  ◇ 6            W       E               ◇ 8 5 3
  ♣ A Q 8 6 4 2        S                 ♣ 10
                      ♠ K 4
                      ♡ Q 2
                      ◇ K Q J 10 9 4 2
                      ♣ J 9
```

On this semifinal deal, Hamman-Wolff sat North-South in the Closed Room, and were opposed by Martel-Stansby. Wolff opened the North hand with a big club, and by the time the auction got back to him, the bidding had escalated to four spades. North-South eventually ended up at the six-level, down two tricks.

In the other room, North opened one heart and East over-called only one spade. Over South's two-diamond bid, West bid only two spades. North-South now stopped in four hearts and scored 420. Certainly East-West needed to do a better job of getting to four spades, and getting there quickly, as they did in the Closed Room.

Let's watch eight of America's finest players battle out a 'four-spades-over-four-hearts' deal from the finals of the 1977 Bermuda Bowl in Manila:

Both Vul.
Dealer North

```
              ♠ A 10 7 3 2
              ♡ 8 2
              ◊ K Q J 4
              ♣ Q 10
  ♠ J                        ♠ K 6 4
  ♡ K 10 5 4      N          ♡ A Q J 9 6 3
  ◊ 10 9       W   E         ◊ 6 2
  ♣ A 8 7 5 3 2    S         ♣ K 4
              ♠ Q 9 8 5
              ♡ 7
              ◊ A 8 7 5 3
              ♣ J 9 6
```

Closed Room

West	North	East	South
Ross	*Soloway*	*Paulsen*	*Swanson*
	1♠	2♡	4♠
5♡	all pass		

Open Room

West	North	East	South
Eisenberg	*Passell*	*Kantar*	*Hamilton*
	1♠	2♡	3♠
4♡	all pass		

In the Closed Room, Swanson made an excellent decision, not only to bid four spades, but to bid it directly. This propelled East-West into five hearts, down one. In the other room, Hamilton chose to bid only three spades at his first turn, and then failed to bid 'four-spades-over-four-hearts'. Sure, there are hands where he would have been right, but following the 'four-spades-over-four-hearts' principle would have been a much better idea, as usual.

Bidding four spades over four hearts is a maxim that some of the world's greatest players have taken to heart. Benito Garozzo seems to be a believer. In the 1975 Bermuda Bowl final he held

♠ K 10 8 6 2   ♡ 7   ◊ A Q 10 7   ♣ 9 7 6

and heard Bobby Wolff open the bidding with four hearts on his right. At favorable vulnerability Garozzo overcalled with four spades! Hamman raised to five hearts, which made in comfort, so the overcall didn't really matter. The point is that the world's best are fully aware of the unusual advantages of bidding four spades over four hearts.

3) WHEN IN DOUBT, BID ONE MORE ON FREAK DEALS

This is something most bridge players learn early in their careers. Some of them misinterpret it to mean simply, 'When in doubt bid one more,' on any deal! Obviously, that would be a gross violation of the LAW. In fact, bridge players in general are more guilty of overbidding than underbidding, especially on partscore hands. The majority of the deals in this book seem to point to such errors of commission. That's because players are forever bidding three-over-three with only 16 trumps, or competing at the five-level with not nearly enough trumps.

The whole picture changes when there is a 'freak' deal. In Chapter Nine we will discuss voids and long suits as *positive adjustment factors*. By this we mean that they will increase the Total Trick count on a deal. We will also introduce the double fit as a factor which inflates the trick count. If there are several voids, and several long suits, not to mention double fits, we can conceivably have a positive adjustment factor of up to four or five tricks!

It's a very unpredictable business trying to guess how many tricks there are on a freak deal. If you think you know how many trumps there are, and how many voids and long suits there are, then good luck! When in doubt, using the maxim of bidding one more on a freak deal is a good principle to remember. Partly, this is because the Law of Total Tricks can't take into account the difficulty of making the correct opening lead. The LAW assumes best play and defense — which implies the best opening lead. On a freak deal the opening lead is often crucial. Rather than randomly trying to guess the right lead, it usually proves safer to bid one more. Let's look at a few celebrated 'freak' deals from World Championship history.

This famous (Bob Hamman would call it infamous) deal comes from the 1980 Olympiad finals in Valkenburg — U.S.A. vs. France:

Both Vul.
Dealer West

	♠ 10	
	♡ K Q 9	
	♢ A 10 9 8 3 2	
	♣ K 9 8	

♠ Q 9 5 3 2		♠ A K J 8 7 6
♡ J 8 5 4	N	♡ A 10 7 6 3 2
♢ Q 6 4	W E	♢ —
♣ 7	S	♣ 2

	♠ 4	
	♡ —	
	♢ K J 7 5	
	♣ A Q J 10 6 5 4 3	

Open Room

West	North	East	South
Perron	*Rubin*	*Lebel*	*Soloway*
pass	1♢	1♠	2♣
4♠	pass	5♣	6♣
pass	pass	6♠	dbl
all pass			

Closed Room

West	North	East	South
Wolff	*Mari*	*Hamman*	*Chemla*
pass	1♢	2♢	2♡
4♠	4NT	5♠	6♣
pass	6♢	6♠	7♢
pass	pass	dbl	all pass

In the Open Room, East played six spades doubled down one, losing a trick each in clubs and hearts. Granted, a club underlead would lead to a heart ruff and down two. In the Closed Room, Hamman led a heart, reasonably enough, against seven diamonds doubled. Declarer guessed trumps, of course, and made his contract!

Just to amuse ourselves, let's see how the LAW works on this deal. Against best defense, East-West can make 10 tricks in spades. North-South can make 12 tricks in diamonds for a total of 22 tricks. There are 11 spades plus 10 diamonds for 21 trumps. However, there are voids, double fits, long suits, etc.

(not to mention that North-South also have 11 cards in clubs, their longest suit, and can easily be held to 11 tricks in that strain). So using the LAW really doesn't make much sense on a deal like this — however, the principle of 'when in doubt, bid one more' unquestionably applies.

The following three-void deal occurred in the first World Bridge Teams Olympiad, held in Turin, Italy in 1960:

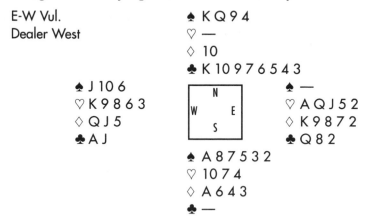

E-W Vul.
Dealer West

♠ K Q 9 4
♡ —
♢ 10
♣ K 10 9 7 6 5 4 3

♠ J 10 6
♡ K 9 8 6 3
♢ Q J 5
♣ A J

♠ —
♡ A Q J 5 2
♢ K 9 8 7 2
♣ Q 8 2

♠ A 8 7 5 3 2
♡ 10 7 4
♢ A 6 4 3
♣ —

When the deal was played in the England vs. United States match this is what happened:

Closed Room

West	North	East	South
Flint	Allinger	Swimer	Mathe
pass	pass	1♡	1♠
3♡	4♠	5♡	5♠
all pass			

Open Room

West	North	East	South
Schenken	Schapiro	Ogust	Reese
1♡	2♣	2NT!!	pass
3NT	4♣	4♡	dbl
all pass			

In the Closed Room, the American North-South bought the hand in five spades. In the Open Room, East's psychic two notrump confused the issue, and here the American East-West bought the hand for four hearts doubled!

North-South can make no less than seven spades — the clubs set up with two ruffs. East-West have 12 tricks in hearts (unless West plays the hand and receives a club lead), losing only to the ace of diamonds. So, this 20-trump deal, with its double fit, long suits and voids produces a whopping 25 tricks! What's the moral? What else — when there is a freak deal, keep on bidding!

4) WHEN YOU HOLD FOUR TRUMPS, CONSIDER MAKING A PENALTY DOUBLE

The 'fourth trump' is a very much underrated phenomenon in bridge. In previous chapters, we've explored the difference between an eight- and a nine-card fit, and seen the significance of four-card support versus three-card support, in terms of the considerable effect these factors have on the balance of the Total Tricks between the two sides. Similarly, four trumps in one hand on defense is quite often a nasty surprise for the declaring side. The 4-1 break will frequently result in their taking fewer tricks than they were planning to. Even when it's only four small, it will repeatedly prove to be a nuisance — causing all sorts of handling problems.

It is that same 4-1 split which takes a trick away from them that adds a trick for us if our side plays the hand. The 4-1 split doesn't reduce the Total Trick count, of course, but it frequently swings the balance one trick in favor of the defending side. If they play the hand, and trumps break 3-2 for them (say we have xxx opposite xx), then our side would have two losers in that suit if we played the hand. However, with xxxx opposite a singleton our side would have only one loser, thus an extra trick. Since the total number of tricks is fixed, one more trick for us on offense means that the opponents will take one fewer trick if they play the hand with a 4-1 break.

Possession of four trumps should, therefore, alert you to the fact that the opponents will be more likely to go down in their contract. This may seem to be just a long-winded way of stating the obvious, but the upshot is that:

Let's take a look at some deals which will illustrate this point. A frequent result of your four-card trump length is that an otherwise normal contract ends up going down several tricks because of the control problems caused by the bad break. This creates an opportunity for a nice profit by making a four-trump double:

N-S Vul.
Dealer East

```
                    ♠ 8 6 2
                    ♡ A 9 3
                    ◇ A J 9 2
                    ♣ 10 9 2
   ♠ A 9 4 3          ┌─────────┐        ♠ K Q J 7 5
   ♡ 10 7 5 4         │    N    │        ♡ 6
   ◇ Q 6            W │         │ E      ◇ K 7 4
   ♣ A 7 5            │    S    │        ♣ Q 6 4 3
                      └─────────┘
                    ♠ 10
                    ♡ K Q J 8 2
                    ◇ 10 8 5 3
                    ♣ K J 8
```

West	North	East	South
McCallum		Martin	
		1♠	2♡
3♡	4♡	pass	pass
dbl	all pass		

On this deal the McCallum team gained 11 IMPs (eventually winning the match by 6 IMPs) en route to the 1985 New York Grand National Team finals. Most West players would be tempted to bid four spades, delighted to have nothing wasted opposite partner's short hearts. A four-trump double should be a standout. Partner can't have a heart void (he'd surely have bid four spades himself), and we can expect declarer to have all sorts of trouble handling the four-one break. In fact, the defense led spades at every opportunity, and declarer could scramble only eight tricks, for -500. The East-West pair at the other table played in four spades, going down one.

Another good thing that can happen when you double with four trumps is that declarer finds himself in a precarious position regarding control of the hand. He may decide against a low percentage line to make the hand if it risks down two or three (especially vulnerable), when he would have been willing to take the chance undoubled. Take a look at this deal from the 1972 World Championships at Miami Beach:

E-W Vul.
Dealer East

```
                    ♠ K 8 4 2
                    ♡ Q 8 5 4 3
                    ◇ 9 7
                    ♣ 4 3
  ♠ A Q J 7 5        ┌──────────┐        ♠ 10 6 3
  ♡ A 10 9           │    N     │        ♡ K 2
  ◇ 2              W │          │ E       ◇ J 8 6 5 4 3
  ♣ A Q 10 7         │    S     │        ♣ 9 2
                    └──────────┘
                    ♠ 9
                    ♡ J 7 6
                    ◇ A K Q 10
                    ♣ K J 8 6 5
```

West	North	East	South
Jacoby	*Forquet*	*Wolff*	*Garozzo*
		pass	1◇
dbl	1♡	pass	2♡
2♠	pass	3♠	pass
4♠	dbl	all pass	

Forquet, thinking there weren't enough trumps in the deck for his opponents to take ten tricks, tried a four-trump double. The East-West hands happened to fit quite well, so it looked as if his double might have backfired. Not so.

Forquet led the diamond nine, won by Garozzo who returned a trump. Jacoby won the ace, crossed to the heart king and had to decide... As we can all see now, if he takes a deep finesse in clubs he'll make four spades doubled. However, if the nine of clubs loses to the jack, North will clear trumps and East-West will be -500. Jacoby, afraid to take that big a risk, decided to make sure of some ruffs in dummy. He led a heart back to his ace, ruffed a heart and played a club to the queen. Now he cashed the ace of clubs and ruffed a club — eventually losing another club and two trump tricks, for down one. The four-trump double may well have created a game swing.

Another good illustration of a fine four-trump double made by Hugh Ross against Hamman-Wolff in the 1977 Bermuda Bowl in Manila can be found on page 222 (Chapter Eleven).

As we can easily see, doubling with four trumps can create a big swing for the defenders. As against that, it will sometimes tip declarer off to the bad break — but I've found that doubling aggressively when holding four trumps is a winning proposition in the long run.

CHAPTER REVIEW

- The maxim *'The five level belongs to the opponents'* says that you'd better know that there are a large number of trumps (usually 20 or more) before you contemplate bidding 'five-over-five'.

- *'Bidding four spades over four hearts'* is one of the few long-run winning actions where taking the push at a high level will pay off.

- *'Bid one more on freak deals'* is a well-founded maxim, and is another exception to the normal rule of not taking a push at a high level.

- *'Doubling with four trumps'* is a long-run winning proposition. A 4-1 break usually means that your side has an extra trick on offense or defense.

CHAPTER 8 QUESTIONS

1) With nobody vulnerable at IMPs, you hear the following auction:

Partner	RHO	You	LHO
1♡	3♣	3♡	3♠
4♡	pass	pass	5♣
pass	pass	??	

You have an agreement that partner's pass is forcing. Should you bid five hearts, or double with the following hands?

a) ♠ A 6 4 3 ♡ A 5 4 ◇ J 10 2 ♣ 7 3 2

b) ♠ Q 7 5 4 ♡ A 10 4 ◇ 3 2 ♣ J 6 5 4

c) ♠ K 7 6 5 ♡ A 5 3 2 ◇ 7 6 4 2 ♣ 3

2) On each of the following hands you are at favorable vulnerability, and your RHO deals and opens four hearts. What should you do, and why?

a) ♠ A Q 9 6 4 2 ♡ A 4 ◇ K 8 3 ♣ 7 6

b) ♠ A 9 8 6 3 ♡ K 3 ◇ K Q 3 ♣ J 3 2

c) ♠ K Q J 9 7 5 3 ♡ 3 ◇ J 10 8 ♣ 10 3

d) ♠ K Q 7 6 3 ♡ A 2 ◇ A 7 3 ♣ A 8 6

3) With neither side vulnerable you hold

♠ K 10 8 6 2 ♡ A Q J 5 4 ◇ — ♣ A 8 5

and open one spade. Your partner raises to two spades, and RHO jumps to five clubs. Partner's raise showed exactly three trumps (Bergen raises). It's up to you.

4) What factors cause there to be more tricks than trumps on a freak deal?

1)   a) Double. You expect at most 18 trumps (if partner has six hearts and one club).

   b) Double. Even though partner rates to have a club void, there are probably only 18 trumps!

   c) Bid five hearts. Here, there is a good chance for 20 or even 21 trumps (if partner has six hearts and one club).

2)   a) Bid four spades. When in doubt...

   b) Pass. I hope there wasn't any doubt with only Axxxx of your suit and a 5-2-3-3 shape. We must have some standards!

   c) Bid four spades. Yes, partner might expect more high cards, but we can't afford to pass with this kind of hand. You will feel terrible if it goes all pass and partner has something like

   ♠ A 5 2   ♡ 7 4 2   ◇ K Q 6 4   ♣ Q 4 2

   d) Double. Four spades could work out, but the spade suit isn't wonderful, and you have tolerance for all the other suits.

3)   Double. Your side has eight trumps. Even if partner has a singleton club (giving them nine trumps), there will only be 17 trumps. To contract for 11 tricks when they have only six makes no sense. In the 1985 Bermuda Bowl, the Israeli South player bid five spades, was doubled and went for -500 when five clubs would have been defeated.

4)   There are three positive adjustment factors, all of which will be discussed in more detail in the next chapter. They are: voids, long suits, and double fits.

MAJOR ADJUSTMENTS

CHAPTER 9

In Chapter Three we looked briefly at adjustments. A good understanding of this concept will, without a doubt, sharpen your decisions when you use the Law of Total Tricks. In this chapter we'll go into the subject of adjustments in more detail.

There is not much literature on the Law of Total Tricks. In the 1960s, Jean-René Vernes introduced the LAW in his book *Bridge Moderne de La Defense.* Vernes researched several hundred World Championship hands, and found that the LAW was 'off' by an average of four-tenths of a trick per deal. (I'm making an over-simplification of his findings — if you understand French and are statistically inclined, you can read Vernes' book to see what I mean!) If Vernes had used adjustments in his analysis, the variance would have been much smaller.

Fortunately, even if the LAW were off by a full trick, we would still be able to benefit from using it. After all, we rarely know the *exact* number of trumps during the bidding anyway — so it's not disastrous if the LAW doesn't work out perfectly on every deal. Still, it's important to be familiar with the adjustments we're about to discuss. Even if you don't plan to make an exact science of the LAW, the principles in this chapter will, at the very least, improve your bidding judgment.

Let's start by considering the following layout of a trump suit around the table:

♠ A Q 3 2

♠ 9 7 4

N
W E
S

♠ 10 8

♠ K J 6 5

On offense, North-South will usually draw trumps in three rounds, and then score their fourth trump in each hand separately, for a total of five tricks. East-West have zero tricks in this suit if they play the hand. So this suit produces five Total Tricks.

Now consider this trump suit:

♠ A 8 3 2

♠ Q J 9

N
W E
S

♠ 10 4

♠ K 7 6 5

This time North-South have one fewer potential trick. They have a third-round loser, and will only take four tricks in the suit. However, this time East-West might take a trick in the suit if they are playing the hand. Sometimes they will be able to make use of the third-round winner (if they have a useful discard), other times the third-round winner will be useless. So in this layout there are either four or five Total Tricks. Let's call it 4½ tricks. (We'll get into the concept of a half-trick later on.)

Let's put these trump suits into complete deals and examine the issue further. Here's a full deal containing the first trump suit we discussed:

```
              ♠ A Q 3 2
              ♡ K 6 5
              ◇ A 9 8 7
              ♣ 4 2
♠ 9 7 4        ┌─────────┐      ♠ 10 8
♡ Q 7          │    N    │      ♡ J 10 9 8 2
◇ K 10 6 5     │ W     E │      ◇ Q J
♣ J 10 9 8     │    S    │      ♣ K Q 7 6
              └─────────┘
              ♠ K J 6 5
              ♡ A 4 3
              ◇ 4 3 2
              ♣ A 5 3
```

Here, the LAW works exactly. North-South have nine tricks in spades (losing one heart, two diamonds, and a club), and East-West have seven tricks in clubs (losing six top tricks in aces and kings), for a total of 16 tricks — equal to the 16 trumps.

Now, let's replace the spades with the second trump suit we looked at above:

```
            ♠ A 8 3 2
            ♡ K 6 5
            ◇ A 9 8 7
            ♣ 4 2
 ♠ Q J 9        ┌─────────┐        ♠ 10 4
 ♡ Q 7          │    N    │        ♡ J 10 9 8 2
 ◇ K 10 6 5     │ W     E │        ◇ Q J
 ♣ J 10 9 8     │    S    │        ♣ K Q 7 6
                └─────────┘
            ♠ K 7 6 5
            ♡ A 4 3
            ◇ 4 3 2
            ♣ A 5 3
```

Now the LAW is 'off' by one trick. North-South can take only eight tricks in spades, because they have a third-round trump loser. East-West still make only seven tricks in clubs — that third-round spade trick is of no use to them on offense. They still have the same six losers in aces and kings. There are only 15 Total Tricks, even though there are 16 Total Trumps.

Consider the following deal, using the same trump suit:

```
            ♠ A 8 3 2
            ♡ 10 9 5
            ◇ 9 8 7 3
            ♣ 4 2
 ♠ Q J 9        ┌─────────┐        ♠ 10 4
 ♡ A K 7 6      │    N    │        ♡ J 4 2
 ◇ 10 6 5       │ W     E │        ◇ A 4 2
 ♣ J 10 9       │    S    │        ♣ K Q 8 7 6
                └─────────┘
            ♠ K 7 6 5
            ♡ K Q 8 3
            ◇ K Q J
            ♣ A 5 3
```

Here, North-South can make eight tricks in spades, losing two heart tricks and one in every other suit. But now East-West can make eight tricks in clubs because the third-round spade winner is useful. No matter what the defense does, East-West will take four club tricks, two heart tricks, one diamond trick, *and a spade*. Thus, each side has eight tricks for a total of 16 Total Tricks and 16 Total Trumps.

So, in this deal the QJ9 opposite 104 of spades provided a trick on offense but, in the deal before, it did not. In real-life bridge hands you can't tell during the bidding whether or not a QJ9 in their suit is going to 'set up' as a useful trick. What you do know is that QJ9 is more useful if it's in your side's suit, as opposed to the opponents'. For example, if your partner opens the bidding with one spade and you're holding QJ9 of spades, these cards are likely to be useful if your side ends up playing the hand in spades.

Holdings such as QJ9 of their suit will usually pull their weight if we end up defending. However, if we play the hand, they produce a trick for us only about half the time.

So what do we do? How do we know how many Total Tricks to count? Sometimes the QJ9 in their suit will cause the LAW to be off by one, and sometimes it won't. This is where the concept of a half-trick comes in. By adjusting our Total Trump count downwards by a half-trick we can be more accurate. There will be many times during the bidding when you'll try to use the LAW, and will conclude that the opponents may have either eight or nine trumps. We simply call that 8½. If, on the same deal, we have QJ9 in their suit, then we reduce the trump (trick) count by one-half, and think of them as having only eight trumps.

The point is not to be bothered by the concept of a half-trick. It's a similar concept to considering

♠ K Q 10   ♡ J 10 8 7   ◇ A Q 10 4   ♣ K 8

worth 15½ points because of the good potential of the spot cards.

In the QJ9 examples we saw that there were two possibilities: either the LAW worked exactly (when the QJ9 pulled its weight on offense), or the LAW was off by one. The direction that it was off is relevant. There were 'not enough' tricks when the QJ9 didn't produce a trick on offense. There were 16 trumps, but only 15 tricks. The QJ9 holding is a 'negative adjustment factor'. A holding of QJ9 in the opponents' suit suggests a *subtraction* from your count of the tricks (trumps). We've already suggested that we should subtract a half-trick because, sometimes the QJ9 will be worth a full one trick, and sometimes it will be worth nothing — the average is one-half.

We have deemed that QJ9 in the opponents' suit represents a *Negative Adjustment* of a half-trick. There are also some factors which represent a *Positive Adjustment*.

The table below lists both Negative and Positive Adjustments. A discussion of each follows.

Negative Adjustment Factors (Suggest Total Tricks will be less than the number of trumps)	Positive Adjustment Factors (Suggest Total Tricks will be greater than the number of trumps)
1) **Negative Purity** minor honors in opponents' suits or poor interiors in your own suits	1) **Positive Purity** no minor honors in opponents' suits or good interiors in your own suits
2) **Negative Fit** misfits	2) **Positive fit** double/double fit
3) **Negative Shape** flat hands	3) **Positive Shape** extra length or voids

NEGATIVE ADJUSTMENTS

Let's start with the Negative Adjustment Factors, all of which suggest that there are fewer tricks than the number of trumps. Keep in mind the significance of there being fewer tricks than trumps — tricks will be hard to come by. Therefore, the LAW will usually guide you to defend (pass or double), instead of bidding on and playing the contract. Negative Adjustment Factors will lead you to adjust the trick count downwards, and will often keep you from bidding on when you shouldn't. This is borne out by common sense — after all, QJ9 in their suit definitely suggests defending as opposed to playing the hand.

Let's look at the first Negative Adjustment Factor on the table, under 'Negative Purity - minor honors in the opponents' suits'. By minor honors we mean queens, jacks and sometimes even tens and nines. We already saw that QJ9 is a Negative Adjustment Factor of about a half-trick. Q10x is another of those holdings that is often a trick on defense, but not on offense. Qxx is not as severely negative as QJ9; however, it too will often produce a trick on defense, but not on offense. Even J9x or Jx could be a nuisance — especially if your partner has the queen.

Later in the chapter, you'll see a chart detailing minor honor problems but, for now, just realize that it is common sense that QJ9 is going to pose more of a minor-honor problem than Qxx. We decided to adjust for QJ9 by deducting a half-trick. For less substantial holdings such as Qxx, or surely for Jx, it wouldn't be fair to also deduct a full one-half.

If you're dreading some long mathematical theorem, don't worry. Yes, we could set up a chart and assign a value to each minor-honor problem, and give everything an assignment out to three decimal places. However, as we already know, it's not necessary to be exact when using the LAW. Why worry about the difference between one-quarter and one-half, when you'll often be trying to figure out whether there are 17 or 18 trumps? All we need to do is to be aware of what is a *negative factor* or a *positive factor*, so that we can decide whether we should lean towards 17 or 18. As you gain more experience with the LAW, you'll see how easy it is to take the adjustment factors into account.

Even a king can be a minor honor. You've probably experienced the following: you have Kx of spades and there is a wildly competitive auction. You seem to have a ten-card heart fit, and the opponents seem to have 10 or 11 spades. The bidding gets up to a high level, and you suspect the ace of spades is on your right (maybe your RHO opened the bidding with one spade). Isn't it often the case that your king of spades is a trick on defense, but is worthless on offense? Perhaps you're just off a few cashing aces, as in the following diagram:

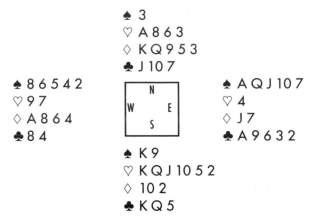

```
              ♠ 3
              ♡ A 8 6 3
              ◇ K Q 9 5 3
              ♣ J 10 7
♠ 8 6 5 4 2                      ♠ A Q J 10 7
♡ 9 7          N                 ♡ 4
◇ A 8 6 4    W     E             ◇ J 7
♣ 8 4          S                 ♣ A 9 6 3 2
              ♠ K 9
              ♡ K Q J 10 5 2
              ◇ 10 2
              ♣ K Q 5
```

On this deal each side has 10 trumps, but there are not 20 tricks. North-South must lose three aces and can make ten tricks in hearts. East-West must lose a trick in every suit, taking only nine tricks, for a total of 19 tricks.

The king of spades is worth a full trick on defense, but is worthless on offense. If East-West sacrifice in four spades against four hearts, South will have to decide whether or not to push to five hearts. If he is able to use the LAW, whatever his estimate of the number of trumps, he will lean towards the lower number because of his king of spades, and will be inclined to defend instead of bidding on.

The next Negative Adjustment Factor is 'Negative Purity - poor interiors in your own suits'. This is just a subset of the minor trump honor adjustment. It tells us that we should be very happy if our trump suit is 'solid' — say, KQ10x opposite AJ9x — but less happy with KJxx opposite Axxx. We must also realize that it is usually a negative adjustment if we are competing in a suit such as K65432, instead of K109876. During the bidding, we will want to make a subtraction from the trick count if we lack interior cards (especially jacks, tens and nines), either in our trump suit or in other key suits we might be planning to use as a source of tricks.

We know that QJ109xx opposite Kx will be a solid trump suit and won't cause any negative adjustments, but that Qxxxxx opposite Kx is a whole different story. Again, we're not going to discuss the exact fractional adjustment you should make for each interior holding. It's sufficient to be aware that J1098x of your suit is much better than Jxxxx. Simply beware of weak holdings such as Axxxx, Qxxx, KJxx, or Kxxxxx in your own suits, and think of adjusting downward.

Here is a full deal where the lack of interiors in the spade suit has a detrimental effect on the trick count:

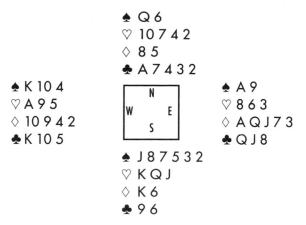

```
                    ♠ Q 6
                    ♡ 10 7 4 2
                    ◊ 8 5
                    ♣ A 7 4 3 2
   ♠ K 10 4                          ♠ A 9
   ♡ A 9 5             N             ♡ 8 6 3
   ◊ 10 9 4 2      W       E         ◊ A Q J 7 3
   ♣ K 10 5            S             ♣ Q J 8
                    ♠ J 8 7 5 3 2
                    ♡ K Q J
                    ◊ K 6
                    ♣ 9 6
```

North-South have eight spades and East-West have nine diamonds, for a total of 17 trumps. Are there 17 tricks?

East-West will lose two heart tricks, along with a trick in each minor, so they have nine tricks. North-South have to lose three spade tricks along with one trick in every other suit, so they have only seven tricks. The poor interiors in spades cause the total number of tricks to be reduced to 16. If the ten (or maybe even the nine) of spades belonged to North-South, there would be one more trick on the deal.

Before we move on to the other Negative Adjustment Factors on the list, let's be sure that we realize which suits these adjustments apply to. Most of the time, 'their suit' refers to their *trump* suit — the suit you expect them to play in. However, it's also important to realize that, if they've been bidding another suit in the auction and you have a holding such as QJ9 in that second suit, that could also suggest a negative adjustment.

Often, you'll know that the opponents have a fit in two suits. Maybe your partner will show the minors and you also have a lot of minors, so you know that they have a fit in both majors. Even though they might be competing only in spades, you know that QJ9 of hearts could represent a negative adjustment.

Problems in the trump suit are crucial — there is no way to 'discard a loser' if that loser is in trumps. On the other hand, a problem in a side suit is only sometimes a problem. Even though a lack of interiors (for example) may subtract a trick from that specific suit, the total number of tricks on the deal may well be unaffected — there still may be enough winners (or pitches) in the other suits that the trick count remains constant. For example:

```
  ♠ Q J 9 7          N           ♠ A K 10 8
  ♡ 5 4          W       E        ♡ A K 2
  ◊ Q 10 9 8         S           ◊ A K J
  ♣ A J 2                        ♣ 10 5 3
```

These two hands produce 12 tricks in spades — the minor-honor problem in the club suit is not a factor.

Now consider:

```
  ♠ Q J 9 7          N           ♠ A K 10 8
  ♡ 5 4          W       E        ♡ A K 2
  ◊ Q 10 9           S           ◊ A K J
  ♣ A J 4 2                      ♣ 10 5 3
```

Here, the minor-honor problem in clubs is probably going to result in only 11 tricks. If the clubs were, instead, AJ102 opposite 543, then there would be a much better chance of 12 tricks. As we already know, AJ10x is a much better or purer holding than AJxx or AJx. It's a problem, or a negative factor, to have empty suits without good fillers. Granted, it won't always make a difference (just look at the examples above), but it's something to take note of.

When deciding how many trumps (tricks) there are, you always want to be aware of the need to make a negative (or positive) adjustment. Be especially alert to honors in their trump suit, but also keep in the back of your mind that, if you have problem or 'unpure' suits such as AJx, you'll probably want to lean towards the lower number of trumps.

Look at the following chart which points out some pure holdings, as opposed to holdings that hint at minor-honor problems.

Minor honor problems	Pure holdings
A J x x	A J 10 9
A Q x x	A Q 10 9
K J x x	K J 10 9
Q x x x	Q 10 9 x
J x x x	J 10 9 x
Q J x	Q J 10
A J x	A J 10
K 10 x x	K 10 9 8
Q 9 x	Q 10 9
J 10 x x	J 10 9 8
J x x	J 10 9
Q x x	K Q J
K x x	
Q x	
J x	

This chart need not be memorized — it's not exact, and it's not even complete. What you should do is think about why holdings such as AJxx as opposed to AJ10x might suggest a Negative Adjustment Factor. If you're trying to decide between 16 and 17 trumps, keep in mind that you might lean towards 16 if your hand is full of minor-honor problems. Think of it as downgrading your hand because you have bad spots.

Also, be aware that, when you analyze a deal from a LAW viewpoint, if it's off by a trick, it will often be attributable to minor-honor problems. As you become a LAW aficionado, you'll no doubt try to convince your friends to use the LAW. They'll love to come running to you when they find a hand where the LAW is off by a trick or two. You'll need a good understanding of minor-honor problems to explain why there weren't enough tricks. You'll also need to read ahead to the Positive Adjustment Factors to see why there will sometimes be too many tricks.

Let's now look briefly at the last two Negative Adjustment Factors on the list — 'misfits' and 'flat hands.'

Misfits are a decidedly negative factor when you're trying to choose whether to bid on or to defend. A look at the East-West hands on the following deal illustrates that there tend to be fewer tricks than trumps if the hands don't fit well:

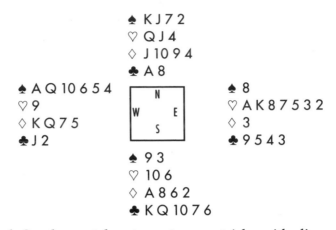

```
                    ♠ K J 7 2
                    ♡ Q J 4
                    ◇ J 10 9 4
                    ♣ A 8
♠ A Q 10 6 5 4        ┌─────────┐        ♠ 8
♡ 9                   │   N     │        ♡ A K 8 7 5 3 2
◇ K Q 7 5             │ W     E │        ◇ 3
♣ J 2                 │   S     │        ♣ 9 5 4 3
                      └─────────┘
                    ♠ 9 3
                    ♡ 10 6
                    ◇ A 8 6 2
                    ♣ K Q 10 7 6
```

North-South can take at most seven tricks with diamonds trumps — they would lose the ace of spades and a ruff, two hearts, and at least two more trump tricks. East-West can be held to only seven tricks in hearts on a trump lead (six heart tricks and the ace of spades). The fact that East and West each have shortness in their partner's long suit results in a shortage of tricks for them on offense. That same factor reduces the number of tricks that North-South take if they play the hand (because East-West can get ruffs).

Our last Negative Adjustment Factor is flat hands, meaning very balanced hands — no singletons or voids. Patterns to be especially wary of are 4-3-3-3 and 5-3-3-2. If your distribution is flat, it becomes statistically more likely that the other players also are flat. If everyone's distribution is balanced, it often depresses the number of tricks. However, flat distribution does not negatively affect the trick count as often as minor-honor problems do. It's merely worth keeping in mind that, if you have a flat hand, and are in doubt about how many trumps/tricks there are, then assume the lower number.

POSITIVE ADJUSTMENTS

We come now to the Positive Adjustment Factors, which will often result in *more* tricks than the number of trumps.

The first Positive Adjustment Factor — 'Purity' — has already been touched upon. Purity means that there are no minor-honor problems, and that we have solidity (good interiors) in our trump suit. Most deals have minor-honor problems in at least one suit; it's extremely rare for every suit to be something like J109x opposite AQ8x, or AKxx opposite QJ10x. If the layout is that pure, there will usually be an extra trick — one more than the total number of trumps.

Let's look at a totally pure deal:

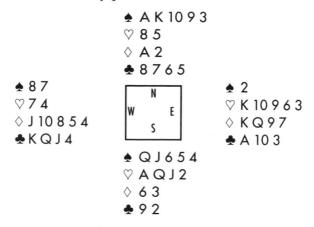

```
                    ♠ A K 10 9 3
                    ♡ 8 5
                    ◊ A 2
                    ♣ 8 7 6 5
 ♠ 8 7                                  ♠ 2
 ♡ 7 4                                  ♡ K 10 9 6 3
 ◊ J 10 8 5 4                           ◊ K Q 9 7
 ♣ K Q J 4                              ♣ A 10 3
                    ♠ Q J 6 5 4
                    ♡ A Q J 2
                    ◊ 6 3
                    ♣ 9 2
```

Here, every suit pulls its full weight, whether on offense or defense. There are no 'either/or' suits like Jxx opposite AQ8x, or Q10xxx opposite Kx.

North-South have 11 tricks in spades, losing only two club tricks. East-West have nine tricks in diamonds for a total of 20 tricks. Yet there are only 19 trumps. The reason for the extra trick is the extreme purity of the deal — nobody has any minor-honor problems in any suit. Look what happens if North's hearts are Jx and South's are AQxx:

```
                    ♠ A K 10 9 3
                    ♡ J 5
                    ◊ A 2
                    ♣ 8 7 6 5
 ♠ 8 7                                  ♠ 2
 ♡ 7 4                                  ♡ K 10 9 6 3
 ◊ J 10 8 5 4                           ◊ K Q 9 7
 ♣ K Q J 4                              ♣ A 10 3
                    ♠ Q J 6 5 4
                    ♡ A Q 8 2
                    ◊ 6 3
                    ♣ 9 2
```

Now the heart suit is not pure. East-West still have the same nine tricks in diamonds. However, North-South have lost a trick from the heart suit and have only ten tricks — the total number of tricks reverts back to the expected 19.

Let's take a look at another pure deal based on a hand which was played in the 1978 New Orleans Olympiad:

```
N-S Vul.                    ♠ Q 10 7
South Dealer                ♡ K 7
                            ◇ K J 10 3 2
                            ♣ A 8 4
        ♠ 8 4                              ♠ K 9 6 3
        ♡ A J 10 6 4          N            ♡ Q 3 2
        ◇ 6 4          W             E     ◇ A 9 7
        ♣ K Q 5 3            S            ♣ J 10 7
                            ♠ A J 5 2
                            ♡ 9 8 5
                            ◇ Q 8 5
                            ♣ 9 6 2
```

Here, North-South have eight diamonds and East-West have eight hearts, so you would normally expect 16 tricks. However, there are 17 tricks. North-South can make three diamonds (nine tricks), losing only one heart, one diamond, and two clubs. East-West can make two hearts (eight tricks), losing two spade tricks and a trick in every other suit.

The reason for this extra trick is the extreme purity of the deal. There are none of those two-way suits such as AJxx opposite Q9x, where the offense has a loser in the suit but the other side doesn't have any tricks in the suit if they play the hand. On this deal, the spades don't produce any tricks for East-West, but they don't produce any losers for North-South. The heart suit also is pure and simple — one trick for North-South whether on defense or offense. The diamonds produce exactly one trick for East-West whether on defense or offense, and the clubs do likewise for North-South.

It's unusual for all four suits to be pure. On the typical deal there is neither excessive purity nor an overabundance of minor honor problems; this results in no adjustments being necessary. We adjust only when things are extreme, either very pure or loaded with minor-honor problems. To make the deal above more typical, let's switch North's ten of spades with West's four of spades to produce this layout:

N-S Vul.
South Dealer

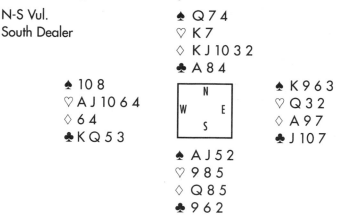

```
                    ♠ Q 7 4
                    ♡ K 7
                    ◇ K J 10 3 2
                    ♣ A 8 4
   ♠ 10 8                              ♠ K 9 6 3
   ♡ A J 10 6 4         N              ♡ Q 3 2
   ◇ 6 4            W       E          ◇ A 9 7
   ♣ K Q 5 3            S             ♣ J 10 7
                    ♠ A J 5 2
                    ♡ 9 8 5
                    ◇ Q 8 5
                    ♣ 9 6 2
```

Now, North-South have a spade loser and so can take only eight tricks. East-West can still take eight tricks, so the total is the normal 16 — equal to the 16 trumps.

You would want to consider adding a trick to your trick count during the bidding if your hand indicates that the deal could be totally pure. Each of the following would suggest purity:

♠ K Q J 8 6 3   ♡ K Q J 10   ◇ 5 3   ♣ 3

You	LHO	Partner	RHO
1♠	2NT	3♡	5♣

Assume you have ten hearts (based on your good hearts you can assume partner has at least six), and they have nine or ten clubs, plus one for purity. You won't consider defending.

♠ K Q 10 3   ♡ 5 4   ◇ A Q J 4 3   ♣ 4 2

You	LHO	Partner	RHO
1◇	2♡	2♠	3♣
3♠	4♣	4◇	4♡

Assume you have nine spades and they have eight or nine hearts, plus one for purity. There are too many trumps for it to be right to defend against four hearts doubled.

The two hands above not only suggest purity, but also incorporate our next Positive Adjustment Factor, which is the presence of a 'double fit.' For LAW purposes, a double fit is defined as: *'Both sides have an 8+ card fit in two different suits.'* Actually, it would be more correct to call it a 'double double fit'. If North-South have an eight-card heart fit and an eight-card diamond fit, that isn't necessarily a double fit. *Both* sides must have an 8+ card fit in two suits.

If East and West are both 4-4-3-2 in that order, we would not consider it a double fit. They would indeed have eight cards in each major. However, North-South would be left with seven diamonds and nine clubs — not meeting the requirements for eight or more in two different suits.

Let's look at a double fit deal:

N-S Vul.
North Dealer

```
                    ♠ A K 5 2
                    ♡ A 2
                    ◇ 7 5
                    ♣ Q 10 9 5 4
      ♠ J 4                            ♠ 7 6 3
      ♡ K Q 6 4          N             ♡ 10 9 8 7
      ◇ A Q 8 3     W         E        ◇ K 10 9 4 2
      ♣ J 3 2            S             ♣ 6
                    ♠ Q 10 9 8
                    ♡ J 5 3
                    ◇ J 6
                    ♣ A K 8 7
```

Here, North-South have nine clubs and East-West have nine diamonds, so there would normally be a total of 18 tricks. Also, North-South have a side eight-card fit in spades, and East-West have a side eight-card fit in hearts — a true double fit.

A double fit suggests a positive adjustment in the Total Trick count. The positive adjustment for a double fit is one full trick so, on the deal above, we would assume there are 19 tricks rather than 18. East-West can take nine tricks with diamonds trumps, and North-South have ten tricks in clubs, for the expected total of 19 tricks.

Just so we don't lose sight of why we use the LAW, let's look again at the double-fit deal above. Assume that North-South are vulnerable against non-vulnerable opponents. North deals and opens the bidding with one club. After East passes, South responds with one spade. Like it or not, West doubles (it usually pays to get into the bidding — especially at favorable vulnerability!). The competitive auction continues up to four spades and East has to decide whether or not to sacrifice. He won't know the exact number of trumps (tricks), but his thinking should go along the following lines...

'My partner has at least four hearts and at least four diamonds, giving us at least a nine-card fit in diamonds, and an eight-card fit in hearts. We have a double fit. What about the opponents? They have at least eight, maybe nine spades. How about their club length? Partner has at most four cards in clubs for his bidding, and I'm looking at a singleton. So, they have at least eight clubs — they too have a double fit.'

So, let's say that we have nine trumps and they have 8½, for a total of 17½. Add one more for the double fit for 18½. We probably even want to lean towards 19 trumps because of the purity of the hand — no minor honors in spades — nice spot-cards in our suits. So, if there are 19 tricks and they're making ten tricks in spades (620), we'll have nine tricks in five diamonds doubled (-300). Using a 'chart analysis,' we'd conclude that it's right to bid on with 19 tricks.

Without accounting for the double fit (or the purity) we'd have come up with 17 or 18 trumps — not enough to warrant sacrificing. Try doing the math for 17 tricks — you'll see that saving will always result in a larger minus than defending four spades.

The last Positive Adjustment Factor is 'Positive Shape — extra length or voids'. This is the logical counterpart of the last Negative Adjustment Factor — flat hands. Unquestionably, the more wild the distribution, the more Total Tricks there will be on a deal. Obviously, a trump suit of AKQJ1098765 opposite a void will produce ten Total Tricks. However, a trump suit of AKQJ10 opposite 98765 might produce as few as five tricks. More realistically, let's think about a trump suit of AKQxxxx. If, based on the bidding, we think that partner has a doubleton in this suit, we would say that we have nine trumps. We know that this trump suit will virtually always produce seven tricks. However, when we have AKxxx opposite Qxxx, it might produce as few as five tricks, or as many as seven or eight (five from length plus ruffs in the short hand). So AKQxxxx opposite xx will usually yield more Total Tricks.

To state it as a rule:

Possession of a seven-card or longer suit is a positive adjustment factor.

For a seven-card suit, you'd probably want to adjust by one-half or one full trick. With an eight-card suit, you'd definitely add one full trick.

Similarly, voids can often be a Positive Adjustment Factor. Consider this infamous bizarre deal which illustrates that it's possible to make a grand slam with as few as five high-card points:

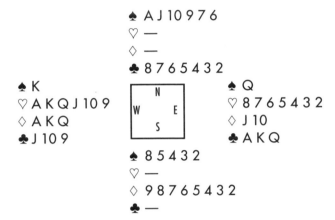

It's pretty silly to apply the LAW on such a freak hand — but let's do it anyway. North-South can take all 13 tricks in spades, and East-West can take 12 tricks with hearts trump, for a total of 25 tricks. There are 'only' 24 trumps, so the LAW is off by one. Notice how the voids and extreme distribution led to there being more tricks than there were trumps.

This is a rather dramatic illustration of why voids can point to making a positive adjustment. If you look at some more normal deals containing voids, you'll see that there will often be one more trick than the number of trumps.

To summarize this chapter on adjustments:

- we expect to have to make Total Trick adjustments occasionally.

- most deals have a few minor-honor problems. Deals with lots of problems will usually have one fewer trick than the number of trumps, and extremely pure deals will often have one more trick than the number of trumps.

- what we want to do in our LAW analysis is to be aware, during the bidding, of factors that might suggest lowering or raising the estimate of the Total Trick count. If we have lots of minor honors, or very flat distribution, we'll subtract. If we have a very pure hand, or extreme distribution, we'll add to the trick count.

Usually, when you count the number of trumps in the bidding, you'll get an indefinite total anyway. You'll often come up with say, '17 or 18'. Depending upon the minor honor situation, you'll be in a position to make an educated guess about which number to use.

If you think about it, adding for purity and subtracting for ugliness is a normal part of most good players' bidding judgment. You'd probably open one spade with

♠ A K 5 4 3   ♡ K J 10 9   ◊ 5 4   ♣ 5 4

— a pure 11-count; but you wouldn't consider opening

♠ K J 5 4 3   ♡ K J 4 3   ◊ Q 4   ♣ J 4

— a minor-honor-filled 11-count. You'd call the first hand 11½ points, and the second '11-minus'. We use the same sort of adjusting to come up with 16½ tricks or '16-minus'.

Keep in mind that, if we can estimate within one trick, we'll usually be able to make the right competitive decision.

- We can never be sure of the exact number of trumps during the bidding. We use adjustments to help us get a more accurate estimate.

- Most deals have minor-honor problems.

- Minor honors are holdings that could produce tricks on defense, but are often worthless on offense.

- There are two types of adjustments:
  Negative — subtract from the trump/trick count
  1) Purity (minor honors, bad interiors)
  2) Fit (misfits)
  3) Shape (flat hands)
  Positive — add to the trump/trick count
  1) Purity (no minor honors, good interiors)
  2) Fit (double fits)
  3) Shape (voids and long suits)

- It is not always clear whether to adjust by one-half or one full trick. We use the adjustment factors to 'lean' towards the lower or higher number of trumps we expect under the LAW.

- We use the concept of a half-trump/trick if:
  a) we think there are eight or nine trumps (called 8½).
  b) we have holdings that will sometimes be a trick, but sometimes won't (such as QJ9).

CHAPTER 9 QUESTIONS

1) What factors should cause you to deduct from the Total Trick count?

2) What factors should cause you to add to the Total Trick count?

3) If there are Negative Adjustment Factors present, what does that suggest you do to the trick count? Does it argue for bidding on, or defending?

4) If there are Positive Adjustment Factors present, what does that suggest you do to the trick count? Does that argue for bidding on, or defending?

5) You think your side has eight or nine trumps, and their side has nine or ten trumps. Assuming no adjustments, how many Total Tricks should there be?

6) After counting the trumps in the bidding, what should you do before thinking about the 'chart'?

7) If your side has a double fit, should you add to the trick count?

8) You think there are 16 or 17 Total Trumps. Approximately what number of tricks should you assume in each of the of the following cases?

   a) The hand is normal — no abundance of minor honors, and no reason to believe the hand is perfectly pure.

   b) There is a minor-honor problem (for example, you have Q10x of the suit they are bidding).

   c) Your trump suit is shaky (for example, Qxxxxx).

   d) You believe both sides have a fit of eight or more cards in a second suit.

   e) You are 4-3-3-3.

f) Your hand is very pure: for example, they are bidding hearts, you are bidding spades, and your hand is

♠ Q J 10 9 8   ♡ 4 3 2   ◇ K Q J 10   ♣ 5

g) You have a seven-card trump suit in your hand.

9) After you count the trumps and make all of the adjustments described in this chapter, will you have identified the exact number of tricks?

CHAPTER 9 ANSWERS

1) Minor honors in their suit.

   Poor interiors in our suit.

   Misfits.

   Flat Hands (4-3-3-3, etc.).

2) Lack of minor honors in their suits and/or good interiors in your own suits.

   Presence of a double fit.

   Voids or long suits — excellent shape.

3) Subtract from the trick count. Defending.

4) Add to the trick count. Bidding on.

5) 8½ + 9½ = 18 Total Tricks.

6) Decide whether there are positive or negative adjustments to be made.

7) Only if the opponents also have a double fit.

8) **a)** 16½ (the average of 16 and 17).

   b) 16 (minor-honor problem — lean towards the lower number).

   c) 16 (poor interiors — lean towards the lower number).

   d) 17 (double fit — lean towards the higher number).

   e) 16 (flat distribution — lean towards the lower number).

   f) 17 (purity — lean towards the higher number).

   g) 17 (very long suit — lean towards the higher number).

9) No! The LAW is not an exact science. After adjusting, you should use the LAW as a guideline — not a guarantee.

IS THERE A DOWNSIDE?

CHAPTER 10

Four of the world's best players were kind enough to look through my manuscript for this book and give their testimonials for the back cover. Bob Hamman had an immediate reaction when I handed him my large stack of typed sheets. Upon seeing the title page, *'To Bid or Not to Bid'*, he chuckled, took out his pen, and crossed out *'Not to Bid'*. Bob's years of experience have taught him that bridge is a bidder's game, and nobody can argue with his glorious track record.

Even though he thought the principles of this book would be of great value to bridge players, he still believes that the LAW has its limits. I agree. On some deals you just don't know how many trumps there are, but that's not really a downside -- you're no worse off than the players who never heard of the LAW. An annoying problem for the LAW user is caused by sheer randomness. Certain suit layouts will affect the trick count for one side and not the other. For example, West is on lead against four spades with Axx of trumps and a singleton club. He leads his singleton and declarer drives out the ace of trumps.

Consider these layouts:

On this layout West can cash only his two heart tricks; East has no entry for club ruffs.

```
              ♠ Q J x x x
              ♡ J x
              ◇ A K x
              ♣ Q J x
  ♠ A x x        ┌─────────┐        ♠ x
  ♡ A x x x x     │    N    │        ♡ K Q 10 x
  ◇ x x x x      │ W     E │        ◇ 10 x x
  ♣ x           │    S    │        ♣ 10 x x x x
                 └─────────┘
              ♠ K 10 9 x
              ♡ x x
              ◇ Q J x
              ♣ A K x x
```

Here East has two entries, so the defense can do two tricks better! If East's hearts were Q10xx, K10xx or A10xx, then the defense could also manage two club ruffs as long as the Jx of hearts was in dummy, and not in declarer's hand. If East's hearts included only one high honor, and no ten, then the defense could obtain exactly one ruff.

The problem with this particular hand is that, no matter how many of the potential club ruffs the defense can actually manage against a spade contract, they'll be able to get all of them in their own heart contract. East-West have nine tricks in hearts on all the layouts discussed. North-South have either eight, nine, or ten tricks in spades, depending upon the location of East-West's heart honors. There are always 18 trumps, but there are either 17, 18, or 19 tricks. The LAW can not take this kind of unpredictability into account.

Another 'downside' (which could actually be considered a corollary) to the LAW is that it breaks down when there are enormous numbers of trumps. If each side has an 11-card fit and 20 high-card points, there are not likely to be 22 tricks. For example:

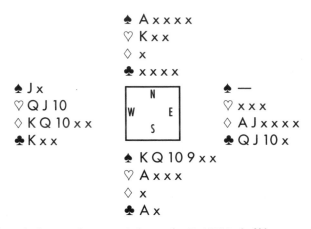

```
                    ♠ A x x x x
                    ♡ K x x
                    ◇ x
                    ♣ x x x x
  ♠ J x              ┌─────────┐        ♠ —
  ♡ Q J 10           │    N    │        ♡ x x x
  ◇ K Q 10 x x       │ W     E │        ◇ A J x x x x
  ♣ K x x            │    S    │        ♣ Q J 10 x
                     └─────────┘
                    ♠ K Q 10 9 x x
                    ♡ A x x x
                    ◇ x
                    ♣ A x
```

Each side has only ten tricks -- the LAW is 'off by two.' When there are more than 20 trumps, then the higher the number of trumps, the less likely it is for Total Tricks to equal Total Trumps. This might be easier to understand if you consider it this way -- if each side had 13 trumps, would you expect that both sides could make a grand slam? Obviously, the more trumps there are, the harder it is to have enough tricks to match the number of trumps.

The LAW's other imperfections can best be understood by looking at an example.

```
Neither Vul.              ♠ 8 2
South Dealer              ♡ K Q 5
                          ◇ Q 9 7 4
                          ♣ Q 9 5 3
  ♠ A Q 10 7 5      ┌─────────┐        ♠ J 9 6
  ♡ 6 2            │    N    │        ♡ J 7 4
  ◇ J 8 3          │ W     E │        ◇ A K 10 2
  ♣ J 6 4          │    S    │        ♣ 10 7 2
                   └─────────┘
                          ♠ K 4 3
                          ♡ A 10 9 8 3
                          ◇ 6 5
                          ♣ A K 8
```

West	North	East	South
			1♡
1♠	2♡	2♠	??

At most tables, the auction would begin as shown above. At this point, South might try for a game, but more likely will bid only three hearts.. He should expect eight trumps for each side, and he can't leave the opponents in two spades with their eight-card fit.

East-West, following good LAW principles, will be happy to have pushed North-South to the three-level and will not bid three-over-three. If East-West were to ignore the LAW and bid three spades, they would do well -- three spades is a down-one sacrifice (-50 or -100) against the cold three hearts. There are 17 tricks (nine for North-South and eight for East-West) due to the purity of the deal. All suits pull their full weight on offense and defense. Unfortunately, there is no way for East-West to know this during the bidding.

Also, if East-West do compete to three spades, North-South LAW followers won't dream of pushing to four hearts with so few trumps. The North-South LAW violators might take the push, and will often be rewarded. If West leads the ace of spades against four hearts, South will make at least ten tricks. In fact, West has to find a diamond shift to prevent an eleventh trick!

This hand illustrates several of the reasons why the LAW won't always lead to the best result:

1) Total Trumps won't always exactly equal Total Tricks. Usually, this is due to the need to make the proper adjustments. Some people know the basics of the LAW, but don't understand when to adjust. That can be remedied by studying Chapters Three and Nine -- but occasionally (as in the deal above) it will be impossible to be aware of adjustments during the bidding.

2) Opening leads. The LAW predicts the number of tricks based upon best play and defense. Best defense assumes that the opening lead will not give anything away. On the deal above, it is quite reasonable for West to lead the spade ace. We make every effort to structure our bidding to help partner on opening lead but, even so, the nincompoop invariably leads from his KJxxx hitting our small double-ton. This results in one or more extra tricks, and causes the LAW to be 'off'.

3) Bad defense. In general, more errors are committed by defenders than by declarers. Common sense alone will tell you that it's two-to-one that either defender will make a mistake, as opposed to just one declarer. And declarer, of course, has the advantage, in that he can see both of his side's hands. On the deal above, it is difficult for West to know to shift to diamonds. As a rule, bridge players tend to be much better at playing a hand than defending -- perhaps because there are more books written about declarer play than defense.

Reasons (2) and (3) both result in extra Total Tricks. Extra tricks argue for bidding on -- not defending. The LAW might tell you that there should only be 16 tricks here, leading you to pass. Meanwhile, in practice, the field will be bidding on, getting a bad lead or a misdefense, and making their contract.

What can we do about this? For one thing, we can bid a little bit more in weak fields. We can expect some poor defense, and we might make contracts that we have no business being in. In a stronger field, we try a little harder to follow the LAW exactly, but still might lean a little bit towards bidding on rather than defending.

Throughout the book, we've seen that the LAW generally takes us in the direction of defending, rather than bidding one more. Most errors in bidding judgment are on the overbidding side. A good working knowledge of the LAW will go a long way toward correcting the problem. My recommendation is that you try to follow the LAW exactly as it is written, with one provision. If you're in doubt (not sure how many trumps there are), then lean towards the higher number. This will often induce you to bid rather than defend, which will, in turn, tend to balance the theory of the LAW with the practical expectancy of imperfect defense and unfortunate opening leads.

THE LAW IN
THE WORLD

CHAPTER 11

Bring your Law of Total Tricks knowledge to the table and tackle these ten problems — all from World Championship play. The players faced with these decisions in the World Championships got only one out of the ten right! Can you do better?

1. Neither vulnerable

♠ J 7 5 4 ♡ K 10 9 2 ◇ A 4 ♣ 10 6 5

You	LHO	Partner	RHO
	1♠	2♣	2♠
3♣	3♠	pass	pass
??			

2. Favorable vulnerability

♠ A K 6 3 2 ♡ 6 2 ◇ K Q 10 ♣ Q 9 7

You	LHO	Partner	RHO
	pass	pass	3♡
3♠	4♣	4♠	5♡
??			

3. Favorable vulnerability

♠ Q 10 4 2 ♡ A J 8 ◇ 8 7 4 ♣ A 8 5

You	LHO	Partner	RHO
		3♣	4♣[1]
??			

1.   Majors.

4. Unfavorable vulnerability.

♠ K J 7 3 ♡ K Q J 6 5 ◇ K 10 ♣ 9 6

You	LHO	Partner	RHO
	pass	pass	pass
1♡	1♠	2♣	2♠
??			

5. Unfavorable vulnerability

♠ Q J 7 5   ♡ K Q 8 7 6 2   ◇ K 7   ♣ 2

You	LHO	Partner	RHO
			1♣
1♡	dbl	2♡	pass
pass	3♣	pass	pass
??			

6. Favorable vulnerability

♠ A 9 6 4 3   ♡ J 6 4 3   ◇ 8 5   ♣ 6 3

You	LHO	Partner	RHO
pass	pass	1NT[1]	2♡
??			

   1.   15-17.

7. Favorable vulnerability

♠ 10 6 5 2   ♡ A K 9 6 5   ◇ 4   ♣ K J 6

You	LHO	Partner	RHO
			pass
1♡	dbl	3♡[1]	4♠
??			

   1.   Weak.

8. Unfavorable vulnerability

♠ K J 2   ♡ A J 10 9 8 3   ◇ K   ♣ 6 3 2

You	LHO	Partner	RHO
1♡	pass	1♠	3♣
pass	pass	dbl	pass
??			

9. Unfavorable vulnerability

♠ 5   ♡ K 9 2   ◇ A K Q J 2   ♣ 9 8 7 5

You	LHO	Partner	RHO
		pass	1♠
2◇	3♡[1]	pass	3♠
pass	pass	4◇	4♡
??			

   1.   Weak.

10. Both vulnerable

♠ K 9 3 2   ♡ 10 6   ◇ Q 10 9 7 6   ♣ 10 7

You	LHO	Partner	RHO
		1◇	pass
1♠	Dbl	1NT	3♣
??			

1) SEATTLE – 1984 WOMEN'S TEAMS OLYMPIAD USA

(North-South) versus Great Britain (East-West)

Neither Vul.
Dealer East

```
              ♠ J 7 5 4
              ♡ K 10 9 2
              ◇ A 4
              ♣ 10 6 5
♠ Q 6 2                        ♠ A K 10 9 3
♡ Q 6 5         N              ♡ J 4 3
◇ K Q 6 5    W     E           ◇ 9 7 2
♣ 9 8 7         S              ♣ A 2
              ♠ 8
              ♡ A 8 7
              ◇ J 10 8 3
              ♣ K Q J 4 3
```

West	North	East	South
Smith	Mitchell	Davies	Moss
		1♠	2♣
2♠	3♣	3♠	pass
pass	4♣	all pass	

North-South –100

In this auction there were two LAW crimes. East's three-spade bid should, by now, be familiar to you as a classic violation. East should have assumed only eight trumps for her side, and had no business competing to the three-level.

The four-club bid was described this way in the *7th Team Olympiad* (the report on the 1984 World Championships published by the ACBL): 'In the Open Room, Mitchell, *expecting spade shortness* (my italics) opposite and probably a better hand, went on to the four-level. This anti-instinctive action was treated shabbily in the result column. After a trump lead Moss lost a spade, a heart, two diamonds and a trump for -100. At least no one doubled.'

Let's think about this in LAW terms. When the three-spade bid came around to North, she should have assumed her partner had one spade and five or six clubs. So the opponents had 8 spades and her side had 8½ clubs for a total of 16½. The minor honor in spades would suggest using 16. By now, you don't need a chart, and you don't have to do much thinking to realize that you shouldn't contract for ten tricks when they have contracted for nine and there are only 16 trumps!

That misconception, 'I have four cards in their suit, so partner is short, so let's bid on', is the source of many bad results. The thinking should go, 'I have four cards in their suit, so there aren't enough trumps, so let's defend'!

2) RIO DE JANEIRO – 1979 BERMUDA BOWL

Italy (East-West) versus Taiwan (North-South)

E-W Vul
Dealer East

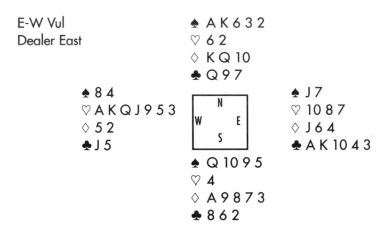

North
♠ A K 6 3 2
♡ 6 2
◇ K Q 10
♣ Q 9 7

West
♠ 8 4
♡ A K Q J 9 5 3
◇ 5 2
♣ J 5

East
♠ J 7
♡ 10 8 7
◇ J 6 4
♣ A K 10 4 3

South
♠ Q 10 9 5
♡ 4
◇ A 9 8 7 3
♣ 8 6 2

West	North	East	South
Pittala	Huang	Belladonna	Kuo
		pass	pass
3♡	3♠	4♣	4♠
5♡	pass	pass	5♠
dbl	all pass		

North-South –300

Italy gained a large swing when the North player from Taiwan failed to use the LAW. You might not agree with the early auction North's three-spade overcall was marginal, as was West's vulnerable five-heart bid. LAW or no LAW, West certainly should have expected to get doubled and go -500 at the five-level with his hand. But it was North's pass of five hearts that was the real crime. Since the opponents were preempting facing a passed hand, and could hardly be bidding five hearts to make, this was clearly a forcing pass situation. North was inviting his partner either to double five hearts or to bid on to five spades. To encourage his partner to bid five spades showed no regard for the LAW. Even if South had as many as five spades, and as few as one heart, there would be ten spades and ten hearts for a total of 20. So, if there were 11 tricks in spades, there would only be nine in hearts — down two doubled for 500 instead of the 450 available in five spades. Most experienced players would probably find the double without using the LAW — but notice how easy this decision would have been for this particular North (who happens to be one of the top players in the Far East) if he had considered the LAW.

In the match, five spades doubled was down two for a 6-IMP gain to Italy, when the other table played four spades undoubled down one. If North had followed the LAW and doubled five hearts, his side would have gained 11 IMPs instead of losing 6 — a 17 IMP swing!

3) VALKENBURG – 1980 TEAM OLYMPIAD

On the following deal, two of the finest players from France and the United States sat West:

N-S Vul.
Dealer East

```
                        ♠ 9 8 3
                        ♡ 9
                        ◇ A Q J 10 6 3
                        ♣ 9 7 6
  ♠ Q 10 4 2                             ♠ 5
  ♡ A J 8          N                     ♡ 7 5 3
  ◇ 8 7 4       W     E                  ◇ 9 5 2
  ♣ A 8 5          S                     ♣ K Q J 4 3 2
                        ♠ A K J 7 6
                        ♡ K Q 10 6 4 2
                        ◇ K
                        ♣ 10
```

Closed Room

West	North	East	South
Soloway	Mari	I. Rubin	Chemla
		3♣	4♣
5♣	dbl	all pass	

North-South +500

Open Room

West	North	East	South
Perron	Wolff	Lebel	Hamman
		3♣	4♣
dbl	4◇	pass	4♡
pass	4♠	all pass	

North-South –100

At both tables East preempted with three clubs, and South cue-bid four clubs to show both majors. At this point, the American

West player in the Closed Room, Paul Soloway, violated the LAW and cost his side a 12-IMP swing. He should have counted nine or ten trumps for his side and eight or nine for his opponents, for a total of 17, 18 or 19 trumps. His minor-honor holding in both of the opponents' majors should have caused him to consider that there were only 18 Total Trumps/Tricks. That being the case, his five-club bid would only be right (and only for a small profit at that) if the opponents had exactly ten tricks for -620, and his side had exactly eight tricks, for -500 in five clubs doubled.

Furthermore, to assume 18 trumps was to allow for the possibility of his partner having seven clubs; however, these days a favorable vulnerability three-level preempt is often based on a six-card suit (particularly in clubs, since there is no weak two-bid available in that suit). On the actual deal there were only 17 trumps, and, not surprisingly, neither side could make anything at such a high level. Soloway is surely one of the world's best players, and his five-club bid was probably a tactical attempt to force North into a bad five-level decision. No doubt, Paul was hoping that his LHO would bid five-of-a-suit, which a player not familiar with the LAW might have done.

The Americans were defeated three tricks in five clubs doubled, and were also defeated in four spades in the Open Room — 12 IMPs to France.

4) RIO DE JANEIRO – 1979 BERMUDA BOWL
Italy (North-South) versus USA (East-West)

N-S Vul.
Dealer West

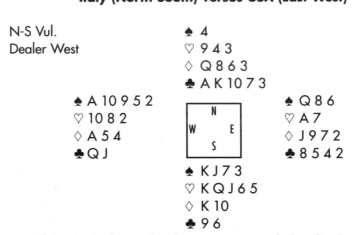

```
                  ♠ 4
                  ♡ 9 4 3
                  ◇ Q 8 6 3
                  ♣ A K 10 7 3
   ♠ A 10 9 5 2                      ♠ Q 8 6
   ♡ 10 8 2            N              ♡ A 7
   ◇ A 5 4       W         E          ◇ J 9 7 2
   ♣ Q J             S              ♣ 8 5 4 2
                  ♠ K J 7 3
                  ♡ K Q J 6 5
                  ◇ K 10
                  ♣ 9 6
```

This deal, from the last segment of the finals, gave the United States a much-needed swing which helped to clinch their exciting victory over the Italians.

In the Closed Room, Italy's DeFalco and Franco (East-West) played in one notrump which was defeated three tricks, +150 to the Americans. Since North-South could probably make +140 in a heart partscore, there rated to be no swing. However, take a look at the auction in the Open Room:

West	North	East	South
Goldman	*Belladonna*	*Soloway*	*Pittala*
pass	pass	pass	1♡
1♠	2♣	2♠	3♡
pass	4♡	all pass	

North-South -100

Although there are only three obvious losers in four hearts, the contract was defeated. Bobby Goldman of the American team led the queen of clubs. Declarer won in dummy and led a spade to his jack and West's ace. Goldman continued clubs and declarer won in dummy and played a diamond to the king and West's ace. Diamonds were continued, and declarer simply had no way to handle all of his spade losers — he finished down one.

The play of this hand illustrates the 'handling problems' that usually materialize when playing in a high-level contract without enough trumps. Certainly, a ninth trump would make this hand much more playable. The ninth trump was 'missing' because South didn't have enough hearts for his competitive three-level bid. He probably figured that his partner was short in spades and thus had some heart length, accordingly, he bid three hearts. There was no need to 'bid his partner's cards'. If South had passed, North would surely have competed to three hearts on his own, and South would have had no reason to bid on to four.

There were only 16 trumps on this deal and the high-card points were pretty evenly divided (22 and 18). This makes it unlikely that one side can take ten tricks. South's three-heart bid with only a five-card suit (not to mention his length in the opponents' suit, and minor honors) was a mistake which would have been avoided if he had used the LAW.

5) NEW ORLEANS – 1978 OLYMPIAD

When Poland faced Brazil in the final, the Polish pair at both tables failed to compete to the level of the number of trumps they held, and it cost them 8 IMPs.

N-S Vul.
Dealer West

```
                    ♠ Q J 7 5
                    ♡ K Q 8 7 6 2
                    ◇ K 7
                    ♣ 2
        ♠ A 9 8          N          ♠ K 2
        ♡ 9 5 3     W         E     ♡ 10
        ◇ A Q J          S          ◇ 8 6 4 2
        ♣ J 10 8 6                  ♣ K Q 9 7 4 3
                    ♠ 10 6 4 3
                    ♡ A J 4
                    ◇ 10 9 5 3
                    ♣ A 5
```

Closed Room

West	**North**	**East**	**South**
Maciészczak	*Chagas*	*Polec*	*Assumpcao*
1♣	dbl	2♣	dbl
pass	2♡	3♣	3♡
all pass			

North-South +170

Open Room

West	**North**	**East**	**South**
Barbosa	*Frenkiel*	*Taunay*	*Wilkosz*
1♣	1♡	dbl	2♡
pass	pass	3♣	all pass

North-South –130

In the Closed Room, the Polish East knew his side probably had at least nine, and maybe ten, clubs — say 9½. (Their one-club opening could occasionally be a two-card suit.) He also knew that North-South had eight or nine hearts, for 8½. That made 8½ + 9½, or 18 trumps. East might have leaned towards 19 because of the extreme purity of his hand. With 18 or 19 trumps it is pointless to defend three hearts. One side has to have at least nine tricks, and, in the actual case, North-South had nine or ten tricks (depending upon whether or not East-West managed their spade ruff), and East-West had ten tricks. East-West went -170 instead of +130.

In the Open Room it was North, again from Poland, who failed to appreciate the LAW. He knew his side had nine trumps, enough reason in itself to compete to the three-level. If he needed any further reason, he should have known that East-West had a substantial club fit, and that there rated to be about 18 trumps (there were actually 19). Selling out to three clubs had to be losing action. Poland fully deserved their 8-IMP loss.

6) SEATTLE – 1984 MEN'S TEAMS OLYMPIAD

The Americans had the home-court advantage for the 1984 Olympiad, but bowed out in the quarterfinals to Austria. This deal was from their round-robin match against Indonesia:

N-S Vul.
West Dealer

```
                    ♠ Q 8 5 2
                    ♡ —
                    ♢ Q 9 6 3 2
                    ♣ 8 7 5 4
   ♠ A 9 6 4 3          N            ♠ K J 10
   ♡ J 6 4 3       W        E        ♡ Q 8 5 2
   ♢ 8 5               S            ♢ A J 10 7
   ♣ 6 3                             ♣ A Q
                    ♠ 7
                    ♡ A K 10 9 7
                    ♢ K 4
                    ♣ K J 10 9 2
```

Closed Room

West	North	East	South
Hamman	Lasut	Wolff	Manoppo
pass	pass	1NT	2♡
2♠	pass	3♠	all pass

North-South +50

Open Room

West	North	East	South
Waluyan	Soloway	Sacul	Goldman
pass	pass	1NT	2♡
all pass			

North-South –200

In both rooms, South was playing poor methods, and had no good way to show clubs and hearts (see discussion of D.O.N.T.

in Chapter Four). In the Open Room, the Indonesian West wisely passed the two-heart overcall and South was defeated two tricks.

In the Closed Room, Hamman should have considered the LAW. (Yes, the LAW is the LAW even for the best bridge player in the world!)He knew his partner had at least two hearts, and therefore the opponents had at most seven. There was no reason to believe that Wolff had three spades, and even if he did — giving his side eight — there would still be only 15 tricks. Either two hearts or two spades would be defeated. The only time two spades would be worthwhile would be if his partner had only two hearts and also four spades. With that hand, he might reopen with a takeout double. On the actual deal, partner had four hearts (admittedly against the odds), and three spades was defeated one trick.

The key point is that Hamman had no good reason to assume the necessary 16 trumps. He needed his partner to have specifically four spades, and only two hearts, for there to be 16 trumps. His length (and minor honor) in hearts should have been a strong warning against entering the bidding. Four cards in the opponents' suit should be a loud advertisement for defending!

7) PORTCHESTER – 1981 BERMUDA BOWL

N-S Vul.
Dealer North

```
                    ♠ A J 7 3
                    ♡ Q
                    ◇ A 9 3
                    ♣ 8 7 5 3 2
   ♠ Q                                  ♠ 10 6 5 2
   ♡ 10 8 3 2          N               ♡ A K 9 6 5
   ◇ 10 8 7 6 5 2   W     E             ◇ 4
   ♣ 9 4                S               ♣ K J 6
                    ♠ K 9 8 4
                    ♡ J 7 4
                    ◇ K Q J
                    ♣ A Q 10
```

West	North	East	South
Munir	**Zanalda**	**Fazli**	**Alujas**
Munir	*Zanalda*	*Fazli*	*Alujas*
	pass	1♡	dbl
3♡	4♠	5♡	dbl
all pass			

North-South +900 (old scoring)

The deal occurred in the Pakistan vs. Argentina semifinal match. Amazingly, at all four tables (the other match was U.S.A. vs. Poland) East-West overreached themselves to five hearts! Do experts think that their judgment is better than the LAW?

In the auction given above, the Pakistani East should figure on nine trumps for his side and eight for the opponents, for a total of 17 trumps and tricks. Even if four spades were making ten tricks, five hearts doubled would go down four. And what if four spades was making 11 tricks? That would be down five in five hearts doubled. And, of course, if four spades was going down — why bid on? All the indications were present to prevent this violation of the LAW.

To add insult to injury, the Argentine pair defending five hearts doubled made East pay the full price. South led a trump, won the spade at trick two and led another trump. He was sacrificing a trump trick, but it was well worth it. Declarer next played a diamond which South won to play his last trump. Declarer was held to his five trump tricks and one ruff in dummy for down five! There were just not enough trumps!

8) MANILA – 1977 BERMUDA BOWL

N-S Vul.
South Dealer

```
                    ♠ A 9 7 4 3
                    ♡ —
                    ◇ Q J 5 3 2
                    ♣ Q J 10
  ♠ 10 8 6 5          N            ♠ Q
  ♡ K Q 6 2      W         E       ♡ 7 5 4
  ◇ 10 9 7 6          S            ◇ A 8 4
  ♣ 8                              ♣ A K 9 7 5 4
                    ♠ K J 2
                    ♡ A J 10 9 8 3
                    ◇ K
                    ♣ 6 3 2
```

Closed Room

West	**North**	**East**	**South**
Ross	Wolff	Paulsen	Hamman
			1♡
pass	1♠	2♣	2♠
pass	3♠	pass	4♠
dbl	all pass		

North-South –200

Open Room

West	**North**	**East**	**South**
Swanson	von der Porten	Soloway	I. Rubin
			1♡
pass	1♠	3♣	pass
pass	dbl	all pass	

North-South +500

On this deal from the semifinals of the 1977 World Championships, two U.S.A. teams faced each other. North-South in the Closed Room contracted for ten tricks, and their

East-West teammates in the other room contracted for nine tricks, a total of 19 tricks bid for. Those sides had, respectively, eight trumps and seven trumps, for a total of only 15. As you could guess, this did not lead to a happy result for the team of Hamman-Wolff and Swanson-Soloway.

Many LAW principles were at work on this deal. Ross made a well-judged four-trump double (Chapter Eight), and Rubin made a good decision to pass the three-level double (Chapter Six). Support Doubles (Chapter Four) would probably have prevented Hamman-Wolff from getting to the four-level.

The decisions of the Rubin team were all in accordance with good Law of Total Tricks fundamentals, and his team was rewarded.

9) STOCKHOLM – 1983 BERMUDA BOWL
France (East-West) versus Italy (North-South)

N-S vul.
Dealer North

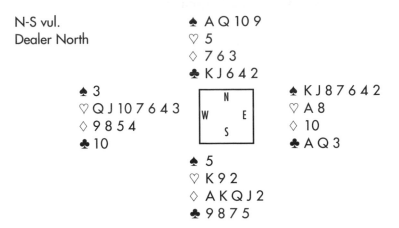

♠ A Q 10 9
♡ 5
♢ 7 6 3
♣ K J 6 4 2

♠ 3
♡ Q J 10 7 6 4 3
♢ 9 8 5 4
♣ 10

♠ K J 8 7 6 4 2
♡ A 8
♢ 10
♣ A Q 3

♠ 5
♡ K 9 2
♢ A K Q J 2
♣ 9 8 7 5

'Mildly offensive to the ear' is how the Open Room auction was described in *The Bermuda Bowl - Stockholm, Sweden – 1983*.

Open Room

West	North	East	South
Lebel	*DeFalco*	*Soulet*	*Franco*
	pass	1♠	2♢
3♡[1]	pass	3♠	pass
pass	4♢	4♡	5♢
pass			
all pass			

1.   Weak.

North-South –200

The reader can decide for himself which of the North-South actions he most dislikes. Without doubt, a knowledge of the LAW would have prevented North-South from contracting for 11 tricks against the opponents' ten-trick contract. There were only 17 trumps, and accurate defense would beat four hearts. Fortunately for the Italians, they were not doubled in five diamonds.

10) BIARRITZ – 1982 ROSENBLUM TEAMS

Both Vul.
West Dealer

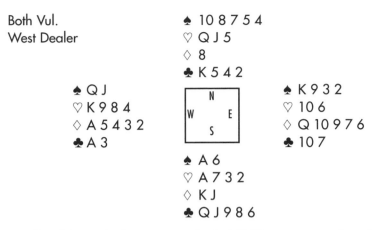

```
              ♠ 10 8 7 5 4
              ♡ Q J 5
              ◇ 8
              ♣ K 5 4 2
♠ Q J                          ♠ K 9 3 2
♡ K 9 8 4         N            ♡ 10 6
◇ A 5 4 3 2   W       E        ◇ Q 10 9 7 6
♣ A 3             S            ♣ 10 7
              ♠ A 6
              ♡ A 7 3 2
              ◇ K J
              ♣ Q J 9 8 6
```

On this typical partscore deal, 6 IMPs were at stake, depending upon which side used the LAW and which side didn't. As you can see, each side can take nine tricks if it plays in its minor-suit fit (there is one loser in each suit for either side). This shouldn't surprise anyone who understands the LAW. There are 19 Total Trumps, but the minor honor problem in diamonds (South's diamonds are worth a trick on defense but are worthless in a club contract) reduces the trick count to 18 trumps — and there are 18 tricks.

In one semifinal match, two United States teams opposed each other. The Rosenblum teams is held every four years, and numerous teams are permitted to enter from countries with large bridge-playing populations. The conditions are set up so that there won't be two teams from the same country in the finals — thus, the two American teams met in the semifinals.

At Table 1, West opened a weak notrump and everybody passed. After a spade lead and a club switch declarer was down one, -100, not a good result since he is entitled to +110 in diamonds.

The Table 2 auction began with more promise for East-West:

West	North	East	South
Chew	Woolsey	Lair	Manfield
1◇	pass	1♠	dbl
1NT	3♣	all pass	

North-South +110

Kit Woolsey (who wrote a praiseworthy chapter about the LAW in his book, *Matchpoints*) made an excellent Law of Total Tricks decision. He knew that his opponents had at least nine diamonds. Ed Manfield had shown clubs and hearts with his double — he probably had at most three diamonds. Kit also knew that his side had at least eight clubs, so there were 17 or more trumps.

Two clubs would seem to be the normal call, but that would make it too easy for the opponents to get the diamond fit into the auction. When they bid two diamonds, Kit would have to push on to three clubs anyway. So why not bid it the first time? He didn't have to worry that his partner would play him for more values — if Kit had a lot of high cards he would simply double one notrump. All jumps like this in competitive partscore deals should be played as 'semi-preemptive.' This is not the kind of auction where North-South are going to bid a game, and there are plenty of other ways to show a good hand if you need to, such as doubling or cuebidding.

The effect of Kit's bid was superb. East should have used the LAW and bid three diamonds (figuring on 17 or 18 trumps), but he didn't. Perhaps he counted high-card points instead of trumps. Woolsey-Manfield scored +110 to cover their teammates bad result.

In the other semifinal match France played Spain, and the Table 1 auction, with Spain East-West, was as follows:

Table 1

West	North	East	South
Diaz-Agero	Lebel	Viedma	Soulet
1◇	pass	1♠	dbl
1NT	2♣	2◇	3♣
all pass			

North-South +110

Here, North survived his failure to jump to three clubs. East bid the expected two diamonds, but West made a poor decision to sell out to three clubs. He had a fifth diamond, and as few clubs as could be expected for his previous bidding. He should have assumed that partner had at least four diamonds (nine or ten for his partnership) and at most three clubs (eight or nine for the opponents). He'd conclude that there were anywhere from 17 to 19 trumps, making it absolutely clear to compete to three diamonds. His timidity resulted in his side scoring -110 instead of +110.

Table 2

West	North	East	South
Faigenbaum	Muñoz	Pilon	Moratalla
1◇	pass	1♠	pass
1NT	pass	2◇	all pass

North-South -110

This time the Spanish player in the South seat was guilty of poor Law of Total Tricks tactics. Here he had no reason to stay out of the bidding and every reason to get in. It is crucial to compete on partscore hands. Look what happens when both sides have a fit and you let the opponents play at the two-level! North-South were -110 in this room, and their teammates went -110 in the other room, for a loss of 6 IMPs. Not surprisingly, this team lost many IMPs on competitive partscore deals, and lost the match easily.

Did you do better than the one-out-of-ten performance of the World Championship participants? Following the LAW should have put you in a much better position than the superstars of the game. Some of the bidding errors on these ten hands (and all deals in the book) could have been avoided even without having LAW knowledge. Surely your reaction to some of the examples was, 'What a lousy bid — it's hard to believe a good player took such an action.' However, none of these errors would have been committed if the players had simply considered the LAW before making their bid.

The examples in this book were chosen to illustrate the LAW at its finest. A good critic can always dig up deals where the LAW would lead to failure. My observations over the past decade have absolutely convinced me that using the LAW leads to success far more often than to failure. Players who are just beginning to use the LAW shouldn't get discouraged when it fails. In the long run your game will be much better with the LAW than without it. For me, it's been the difference between winning and losing!

APPENDICES

Glossary

Adjustments Addition to or subtraction from the Total Trick count to allow for minor honor problems, purity, etc.

Balancing Seat The position occupied by the player who can end the auction by passing.

Bergen Raises Conventional means of raising a one-heart or one-spade opening to the proper LAW level.

Bermuda Bowl The World Team Championships which are held every odd-numbered year.

Chart Used in this book to mean a table of scores for each number of Total Tricks for both sides.

Competitive Bidding Bidding in contested auction, i.e. both sides are in the bidding.

Direct Seat The position occupied by the player whose turn it is to bid, immediately after his RHO has bid.

D.O.N.T. Conventional method for interfering against 1NT as described in Chapter Four.

Double-dummy Playing (or analyzing) a deal as if all four hands are in view.

Drury Conventional method for a passed hand to show a good raise of a major-suit opening (Chapter Four).

Duplicate Scoring Scoring method used in modern-day bridge tournaments. See Appendix A.

Favorable Vulnerability The vulnerability at which your side is not vulnerable against vulnerable opponents.

Good-Bad 2NT Conventional method (similar to Lebensohl) for competing at the three-level (Chapter Five).

Half-trick Used as part of the adjusting process to help in rounding to the proper number of Total Tricks.

IMPs International Match Points. Method of scoring used in most team matches and some pairs games. See Appendix B.

Jacoby Transfers Conventional method of responding to 1NT which is discussed in Chapter Four.

LAW Protection The concept that dictates that it's safe to bid to the level of the number of trumps held by the partnership.

Lebensohl A conventional method to show a weak three-level bid by relaying first with 2NT.

LHO Left-hand opponent.

Matchpoints Scoring method whereby you receive one point for each pair that you score better than on a deal. Duplicate Scoring is used (see Appendix A).

Minor Honors Holdings such as QJx or Q10x in the opponents' suits which will often provide a trick on defense, but not on offense.

Mixed Raise More than a preemptive raise, but less than a limit raise.

Nationals Tournaments held three times a year in North America in which the world's best players compete.

Negative Adjustments The factors (discussed in Chapters Three and Nine) which cause you to lower the estimate of the number of Total Tricks.

OBAR Bids Systemic approach to allow for 'Balancing In Direct Seat after the Opponents Bid And Raise'. (Chapter Five)

Olympiad World Pairs and Teams Championships held every four years.

Precision Bidding system invented by C.C. Wei which employs the use of a strong artificial one-club opening.

Positive Adjustment The factors (discussed in Chapters Three and Nine) which cause you to add to the estimate of the number of Total Tricks.

Pure/purity The condition of a deal in which there are no minor-honor problems. All suits pull their full weight on offense or defense, and usually suggest a positive adjustment.

Reisinger National Team Championship held at the Fall Nationals which is scored 'board-a-match'.

Responsive Double A double, after your partner has doubled, to show high cards but no biddable suit.

RHO Right-hand opponent.

Rosenblum Cup World Championship Teams event held every four years.

Scrambling 2NT Systemic approach whereby 2NT is used as an artificial way to 'scramble' into the correct contract (Chapter Five).

Soft Holding Holdings such as QJx or J9xx which will produce 'slow' tricks.

Spingold National Team knockout event held at the Summer Nationals.

Strain The denomination of the final contract (spades, hearts, diamonds, clubs, or notrump).

Super-Acceptance A jump in response to a transfer bid.

Support Doubles Conventional method to show partner three-card support for the suit he has responded in (Chapter Four).

Swiss Teams Popular form of Teams event scored by IMPs.

Team game Knockout or Swiss match between teams of at least four players. All references in this book imply duplicate scoring and IMPs.

Team Trials Event held once a year in Memphis to determine the U.S. team representatives for the World Championships.

Total Tricks The total number of tricks that both sides can make if each plays in its longest trump fit.

Total Trumps The total number of trumps on a deal using both partnerships' longest trump fit.

Unfavorable Vulnerability The vulnerability at which your side is vulnerable against non-vulnerable opponents.

Unusual NT The use of a 1NT or 2NT overcall to show two suits (usually the two lowest unbid).

Vanderbilt National Team knockout event held at the Spring Nationals.

Venice Cup Women's World Team Championship held every odd-numbered year.

VuGraph Closed circuit broadcast of an important bridge game to a viewing audience.

APPENDIX A — DUPLICATE SCORING

Bid	Made	Not Vul. Reg.	Dbld.	Vul. Reg.	Dbld.
1 Minor	1	70	140	70	140
	2	90	240	90	340
	3	110	340	110	540
	4	130	440	130	740
	5	150	540	150	940
	6	170	640	170	1140
	7	190	740	190	1340
1 Major	1	80	160	80	160
	2	110	260	110	360
	3	140	360	140	560
	4	170	460	170	760
	5	200	560	200	960
	6	230	660	230	1160
	7	260	760	260	1360
1NT	1	90	180	90	180
	2	120	280	120	380
	3	150	380	150	580
	4	180	480	180	780
	5	210	580	210	980
	6	240	680	240	1180
	7	270	780	270	1380
2 Minor	2	90	180	90	180
	3	110	280	110	380
	4	130	380	130	580
	5	150	480	150	780
	6	170	580	170	980
	7	190	680	190	1180
2 Major	2	110	470	110	670
	3	140	570	140	870
	4	170	670	170	1070
	5	200	770	200	1270
	6	230	870	230	1470
	7	260	970	260	1670
2NT	2	120	490	120	690
	3	150	590	150	890
	4	180	690	180	1090
	5	210	790	210	1290
	6	240	890	240	1490
	7	270	990	270	1690
3 Minor	3	110	470	110	670
	4	130	570	130	870
	5	150	670	150	1070
	6	170	770	170	1270
	7	190	870	190	1470
3 Major	3	140	530	140	730
	5	460	750	660	1150
	6	490	850	690	1350
	7	520	950	720	1550
	4	170	630	170	930
	5	200	730	200	1130
	6	230	830	230	1330
	7	260	930	260	1530
3NT	3	400	550	600	750
	4	430	650	630	950
	5	460	750	660	1150
	6	490	850	690	1350
	7	520	950	720	1550

Bid	Made	Not Vul. Reg.	Dbld.	Vul. Reg.	Dbld.
4 Minor	4	130	510	130	710
	5	150	610	150	910
	6	170	710	170	1110
	7	190	810	190	1310
4 Major	4	420	590	620	790
	5	450	690	650	990
	6	480	790	680	1190
	7	510	890	710	1390
4NT	4	430	610	630	810
	5	460	710	660	1010
	6	490	810	690	1210
	7	520	910	720	1410
5 Minor	5	400	550	600	750
	6	420	650	620	950
	7	440	750	640	1150
5 Major	5	450	650	650	850
	6	480	750	680	1050
	7	510	850	710	1250
5NT	5	460	670	660	870
	6	490	770	690	1070
	7	520	870	720	1270
6 Minor	6	920	1090	1370	1540
	7	940	1190	1390	1740
6 Major	6	980	1210	1430	1660
	7	1010	1310	1460	1860
6NT	6	990	1230	1440	1680
	7	1020	1330	1470	1880
7 Minor	7	1440	1630	2140	2330
7 Major	7	1510	1770	2210	2470
7NT	7	1520	1790	2220	2490

DEFEATED CONTRACTS

DOWN:	Not Vul.		Vul.	
1	50	100	100	200
2	100	300	200	500
3	150	500	300	800
4	200	800	400	1100
5	250	1100	500	1400
6	300	1400	600	1700
7	350	1700	700	2000
8	400	2000	800	2300
9	450	2300	900	2600
10	500	2600	1000	2900
11	550	2900	1100	3200
12	600	3200	1200	3500
13	650	3500	1300	3800

APPENDIX B - IMP TABLE

Diff. In Pts.	IMPs	Diff. in Pts.	IMPs
20-40	1	750-890	13
50-80	2	900-1090	14
90-120	3	1100-1290	15
130-160	4	1300-1490	16
170-210	5	1500-1740	17
220-260	6	1750-1990	18
270-310	7	2000-2240	19
320-360	8	2250-2490	20
370-420	9	2500-2990	21
430-490	10	3000-3490	22
500-590	11	3500-3990	23
600-740	12	4000 and up	24

PLAYER INDEX

BIBLIOGRAPHY

The Law of Total Tricks by Jean Rene
Vernes in 'Bridge World,' June,
1969 — 144
The Bridge World – PO Box 299
Scarsdale, NY 10583

Better Bidding with Bergen By Marty
Bergen, Volume I & II — 64, 69, 83,
101, 102
Published by Devyn Press, Inc.
3600 Chamberlain Lane, Suite 230
Louisville, Kentucky 40241

Bridge Moderne de La Defense 1966 by
Jean-Rene Vernes — 144, 176

Master Solvers Column 'The Bridge
World' December, 1991 — 141

Matchpoints by Kit Woolsey — 226
Published by Devyn Press, Inc.

Sunday New York Times Bridge Column
May, 1984 By Alan Truscott — 119

The Official Encyclopedia of Bridge
ACBL — 2990 Airways Boulevard
Memphis, Tennessee 38116

ABOUT THE AUTHOR

Larry Cohen was born 4/14/59 in New York City, but now resides with his wife, Maria, in Boca Raton, Florida.

Formerly a computer programmer and options trader, he presently makes his living from lecturing, writing/publishing bridge books, articles and software, and playing bridge professionally. His biggest passions are golf and watching sports, especially his beloved Yankees.

He learned to play bridge at age 6 from his grandparents, started playing duplicate at age 14, and became a Life Master at 17. He won his first National Championship at age 22 and can now count 17 national titles among his successes (see below).

Larry is Director of the prestigious *Bridge World* Master Solvers Club, a National Appeals Committee Member and panelist and a former chairman of the ACBL Hall-of-Fame Committee. His books include the best-selling *To Bid or Not to Bid, Following the LAW,* and *Larry Cohen's Bidding Challenge.*

CAREER DETAILS

1981 Won Spingold	**1992** Won Pan-American Open Teams
1981 Won Blue Ribbon Pairs	
1983 Won Cavendish Invitational Pairs	**1993** Semi-Final Bermuda Bowl, Santiago
1983 Won Blue Ribbon Pairs	**1993** Placed 2nd in Vanderbilt
1983 Placed 2nd in Spingold	**1995** Won Grand National Teams
1983 Won Life Master Mens Pairs	**1996** Won Blue Ribbon Pairs
1984 Won Spingold	**1996** Won National Open Pairs
1984 Won National Mens BAM	**1996** Won Life Master Pairs
1985 Won Reisinger	**1998** Placed 2nd in US Team Trials
1987 Won Life Master Pairs	**1998** Second in World Open Pairs, Lille
1988 Won Cavendish Invitational Pairs	**1999** Won the Cap Gemini in the Hague
1988 Won Blue Ribbon Pairs	**1999** Won North American Swiss Teams
1988 Won Life Master Pairs	
1990 Placed 2nd in Vanderbilt	**2000** Won U.S. Team Trials
1990 Won the Fall Open BAM	**2000** Bronze Medal Olympiad, Maastricht
1991 Won Reisinger	
1991 Won the Fall Open BAM	**2002** 2nd U.S. Team Trials
1991 Second North American Open Teams	